Finance for Small and Medium-sized Enterprises in the Caribbean

Erwin E. Brewster

COMMONWEALTH SECRETARIAT

Commonwealth Secretariat, Marlborough House, Pall Mall
London SW1Y 5HX, United Kingdom

Economic Paper 76 in the Commonwealth Economic Paper Series

Published by the Commonwealth Secretariat

Designed by Wayzgoose
Printed by Hobbs the Printers Ltd, Totton, Hampshire

Copies of this publication may be obtained from
The Publications Section, Commonwealth Secretariat,
Marlborough House, Pall Mall, London SW1Y 5HX,
United Kingdom
Tel: +44 (0)20 7747 6342
Fax: +44 (0)20 7839 9081

E-mail: publications@commonwealth.int
Web: www.thecommonwealth.org/publications

ISBN-10: 0-85092-843-5
ISBN-13: 978-0-85092-843-3

Contents

Appendices

Figures

Tables

Appendix 2

Acknowledgements

The survey and this report have greatly benefited from discussions with the following people:

Carol Ayoung, Caribbean Association of Industry and Commerce
Havelock Brewster, Inter-American Development Bank
Doreen De Caries, Guyana Manufacturers' Association
Prakash Dhanrajh, Development Finance Ltd
Jocelyn Dow, Liana Cane Interior Ltd
F. Fletcher, Adventure Manufacturing Company Ltd, Guyana
Malcolm Hately, Development Finance Bank South America
Imtiaz Hosein, Business Development Company Ltd
Jonathan Lashley, University of the West Indies – Cave Hill
Anthony Maughan, Caribbean Development Bank
Stanley Odle (Consultant)
Paul Quesnel, Trinidad & Tobago Manufacturers Association

Special thanks to Professor Andreas Antoniou and Cheryl Bruce of the Commonwealth Secretariat for their support and encouragement throughout the project.

I also wish to acknowledge the work and efforts of the researchers who assisted on this project.

Introduction

This attempt by the Commonwealth Secretariat to analyse the problems confronting small and medium-sized enterprises (SMEs) in their efforts to access long-term finance is intended to address the basic proposition that the main opportunities for development and increased employment in the Caribbean lie in the expansion of this sector. The sector has been widely recognised as the engine of economic growth and as the area that holds out most promise for the economic development of the CARICOM (Caribbean Community and Common Market) countries. This is particularly so now that the major engines of economic activity in developing countries are threatened by world free trade protocols and economic globalisation.

The objective of the study was to ascertain whether or not SMEs had adequate access to long-term finance and, if not, what the obstacles were to such access. Access in this context is taken to mean not only the availability of finance, but also the ability of SMEs to satisfy the market requirements under which finance is made available. The study also sought to identify the obstacles to the growth of SMEs, and their requirements for development and expansion. To this end, the inquiry sought to solicit from SMEs their perceptions on several issues relevant to their financing needs, and their views on what could be done to further their interests and by whom. The study was initiated after it became evident that there was a need for something to be done to accelerate the growth of SMEs in the Caribbean. It was felt that, despite their importance, SMEs continued to face problems in realising their potential for growth. In the context of recent studies on how to lower the threshold,[1] the Commonwealth Secretariat was concerned about the problems facing SMEs and recognised the need for the implementation of measures to ensure the survival and growth of the sector.

Unfortunately, because no database exists on Caribbean enterprises (although individual countries have databases in various stages of completeness), it has not been possible to evaluate a random sample of SMEs across the Caribbean. The survey does not, therefore, purport to sample the whole population of SMEs in the Caribbean. Rather, a number of businesses answering to a pre-determined description of small and medium-sized enterprises were selected from ten CARICOM countries for examination. These operate in a spread of economic sectors in which new enterprises are often set up. The aim of the study was to test the experiences of these businesses in their attempts to secure long-term finance and to expand or develop.

Although the survey is restricted in scope to examining the difficulties encountered by such enterprises in accessing long-term finance and how these can be overcome, it

1 Anthony Hughes and Havelock Brewster (2001). *Lowering the Threshold – Reducing the Cost and Risk of Private Direct Investment in Least Developed, Small and Vulnerable Economies*. London: Commonwealth Seretariat.

sheds light on wider issues. A general difficulty in soliciting information is the lack of any legislation requiring business enterprises to subscribe to officially sponsored surveys. For example, none of the commercial banks approached in Antigua or Barbados would participate in the survey. Some strengthening of the law in all the countries of the CARICOM area is needed if any meaningful information is to be adduced about the state of the economy and if plans are to be made for improvement in any given direction.

The experience, however, has been an enlightening one. Curiously, no two countries have the same definition of 'small and medium-sized enterprises'; nor did any of the many development agencies agree on what constituted 'small and medium-sized'. It was necessary, therefore, first to develop a definition that did not deviate too greatly from what appeared to be a general understanding of the nature of such businesses, but at the same time took into account some of the realities of the variation in economic circumstances within the region. This question is dealt with in Appendix 1.

The researchers in the field reported many problems in gaining the support of the businesses which were asked to respond to the questionnaire. These ranged from outright refusal to the problem of not having adequate information to permit a response to be made. Financial institutions were particularly reticent and could not be drawn out on even the more innocuous aspects of their business relationships with their clients. For example, few responded to the question whether they kept records of the number of employees of their business clients: perhaps they did not routinely maintain such records. Similarly, few responded to the question on how many requests for finance were received in the last five years. Surprisingly, some businesses were very willing to participate and offered their information freely and frankly. Others, however, were very concerned about the use to which the information could be put and whether their disclosures might expose them to security risks. These businesses were naturally more reluctant to divulge any information of a financial nature. Of a total of more than 200 targeted SMEs, 125 responded in a manner that could be regarded as reasonably complete, while of the nearly 60 financial institutions approached, 32 attempted to respond fully.

In discussions with established business associations, i.e. chambers of commerce and employers' associations, there appeared to be little if any empathy with any organisation that fell outside their membership criteria. There is therefore little interest in assisting smaller enterprises outside the terms of reference of these associations. To an extent this is understandable, as these organisations are often financially challenged in supporting even their own activities, which are mostly confined to lobbying government in their own interests. Even with the best intentions, there is little they are able or prepared to do to support SMEs that fall outside their structures.

Most SMEs do not know the extent, if any, of the support they can expect to receive from government and do not enquire except in cases of dire emergency, as in Guyana after the flooding on the east coast in 2006 caused damage to many small businesses. There was a feeling in some quarters that resources were made available, even by banks, on a selective basis for partisan reasons and not on any objective assessment of the viability of the enterprises that needed them.

Executive Summary

The study is presented in four parts. The first sets out the contextual circumstances of the SMEs surveyed on several parameters, and provides the background to the survey. There is no information on how many SMEs operate in any one country despite legal requirements for the registration of companies and trade names. It is therefore not possible to assess the statistical significance of the sample. The personal characteristics of the owners of these businesses are also presented with a view to determining if they impact on the success of the businesses in accessing finance. The first section provides the context of the survey and gives a brief insight into the types of businesses that make up the SME sector, the range of legal forms and sizes they represent, and the characteristics of their owners.

The second part examines the attempts of SMEs to access long-term finance, and indeed finance of any nature, and their experiences in this regard. 'Long-term finance' was defined for the purposes of the survey as finance for a term of more than ten years. No attempt is made to evaluate the responses and they are presented as an account of the experiences of the businesses that responded to the questionnaires.

The third part presents the perceptions of SMEs as a whole in their attempts to deal with the financial environment; it attempts to extrapolate from these perceptions the more generally felt assumptions in their struggle to achieve some level of financial viability. Using the findings of the survey, the nature of the relationships between SMEs and their environment, including both business and government, will be assessed. The main opportunities for the improvement and expansion of the sector are identified in so far as they are supported by the findings of the survey, and a way forward is indicated.

The fourth part deals with the reactions and perceptions of lenders to requests by SMEs for finance, including long-term finance. The study examines the types of finance most often requested from financial institutions, the range of finance requested, and the nature of the evaluation and decision-making processes. It also looks at the views of lenders on opportunities for risk sharing.

In conclusion, some observations are offered as to the way forward to alleviate some of the major difficulties faced by SMEs and to assist in energising the sector.

The survey covered 125 businesses in ten CARICOM countries and 12 business sectors. It examined the number of employees, revenue, assets, origins, growth rates and years in business. The age, educational qualifications, gender and managerial experience of the owners of the businesses were also taken into account.

The majority of the businesses had between six and 25 employees and assets of less than US$100,000. Fifteen per cent of the businesses were owned by women, and a further 12 per cent had joint male and female ownership. The majority of owners were over 40 years old and held university degrees.

Seventy-eight of the 125 businesses had applied for long-term finance in the last three years, of which 68 per cent had been successful. Thirteen per cent sought equity finance and 15 per cent sought a government grant.

The main providers of credit are banks, followed by credit unions. The main reason why some businesses did not seek finance was because they did not need it. They also felt that the cost of finance was too high. In the majority of cases where financing was successful, owners had to provide personal assets as collateral and in many cases business assets as well.

The majority of businesses feel that the maximum finance they need is less than US$100,000 for a term of less than ten years. The main purposes for which the finance would be used are to purchase machinery and equipment and for product development.

SMEs feel that the major obstacle to their development is the high cost of finance and the most appropriate finance for their business is long term. The majority did not have any difficulty in completing the application process for finance, but those that did have difficulty felt that too much information was requested.

SMEs reported that the main problem encountered in their businesses was the lack of access to long-term finance, followed by the shortage of skilled labour. Less than one-third had attended a managerial training programme; managers would avail themselves of such programmes if they were offered at affordable rates.

Lenders for their part seem willing to provide funds to SMEs but only where they meet the strict risk evaluation criteria employed and are prepared to pay the going rate. Their perception of how well they perform in this regard differs somewhat from that of SMEs.

The concerns expressed by SMEs and organisations which represent their interests reflect not only a lack of access to long-term finance, but also a lack of access to any form of affordable finance. It was generally accepted that finance was far too expensive and that they would be better off relying on their own resources. The need for collateral, the lack of liquidity and the low net worth of businesses are major impediments to access to any form of finance. That long-term finance might be made cheaper does not appear to have been given any serious consideration. Most SMEs look to their governments to alleviate the burdens, financial or otherwise, that they encounter on the path to development. Commercial banks are not considered to be sympathetic partners in this process, although they are the most favoured source of finance. Most SMEs feel that governments should do more to facilitate access to long-term finance, and that they should reduce taxation and publish more relevant information.

1 Contextual Data Analysis

The study examines SMEs on a number of parameters, including employee size, turnover, assets, legal status, years in business, growth rates, and product or service type. A full tabulation of business characteristics is set out in Table A1.1 of Appendix 2. The personal characteristics of the owners of the businesses were also examined by age, business experience, management experience, gender and highest educational level. A tabulation of the characteristics of principal owners is given in Table A1.2 of Appendix 2.

A specific attempt was made to exclude businesses that might fall within the micro-enterprise category, i.e. businesses with less than five employees. However, this was not always possible, especially in smaller countries such as Grenada and St Lucia, where the majority of small businesses employ between one and five people.

Smaller businesses are, as is to be expected, more numerous than larger ones, although this may also have been the result of self-selection in the sense that many of the larger businesses declined to participate in the survey.

1

Business Characteristics

Figure 1.1 shows that the majority of businesses surveyed (56%) employed between six and 25 workers, while about 20 per cent employed between 26 and over 100. Twenty-six per cent employed fewer than six people. Table A1.3 of Appendix 2 shows the distribution of businesses by number of employees according to product type, and Tables A1.4 and A1.5 show the distribution by years in business and sales growth in the last two years.

Figure 1.1: Distribution of Businesses by Number of Employees

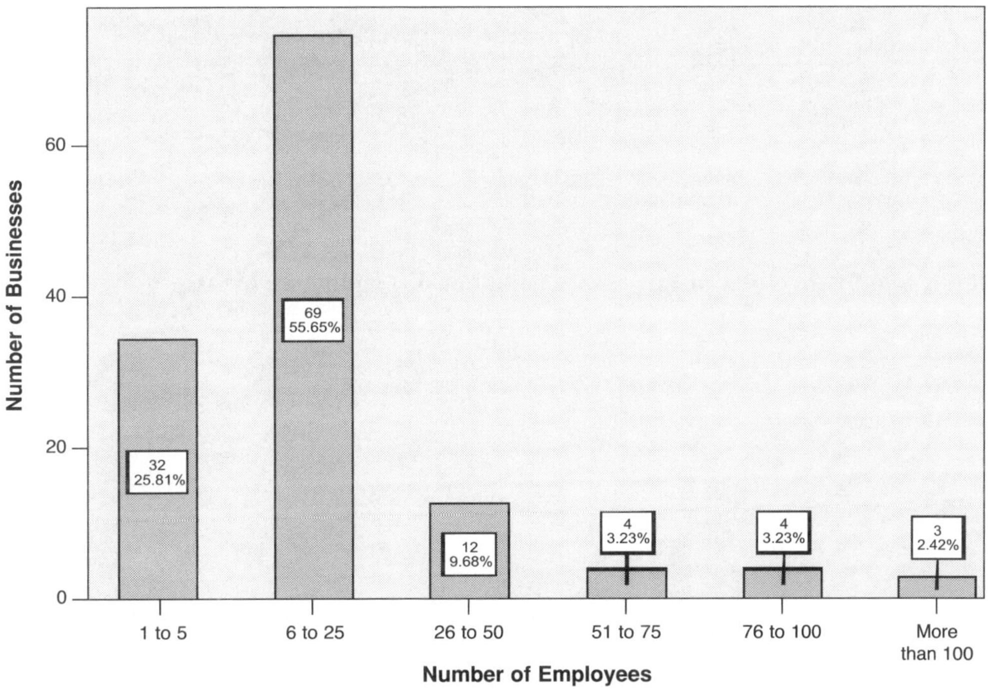

Figures 1.2 and 1.3 show the distribution of businesses by revenue and assets. Just under one-third of businesses had annual revenue and assets of less than US$100,000. However, a surprisingly large number (17.7%) fell into the category of businesses which had more than US$1 million in revenue.

Figure 1.4 shows that the businesses making up the greater part of the survey were in the services (29.6%), distribution (13.6%), food processing (12.8%) and hospitality (11.2%) sectors. Building material, construction, machinery and manufacturing were represented by 8 per cent of the businesses surveyed. These figures accord with the general

Figure 1.2: Distribution of Businesses by Revenue

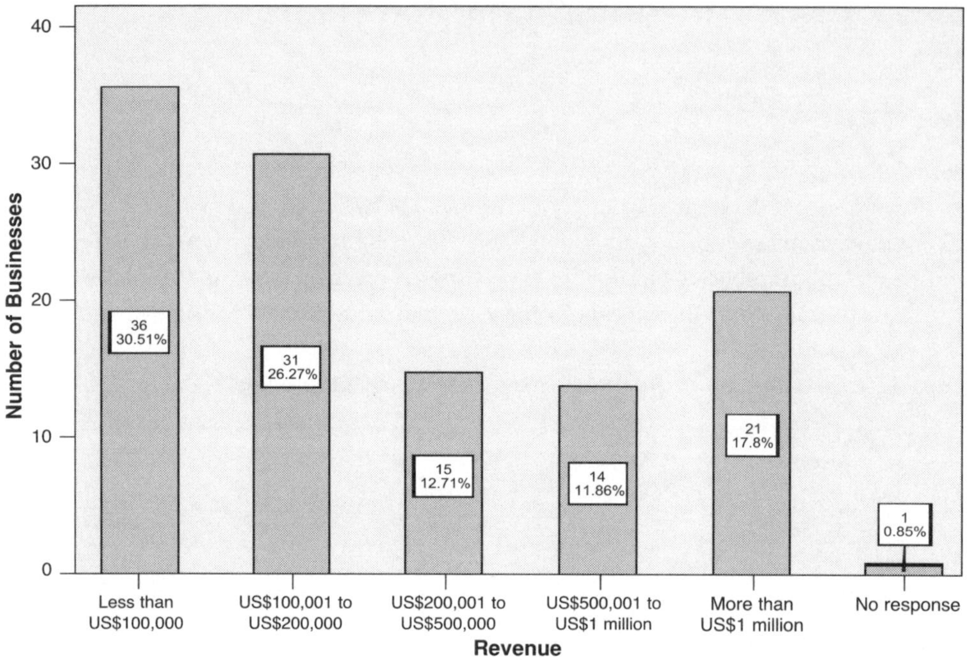

Figure 1.3: Distribution of Businesses (Number of Employees) by Assets

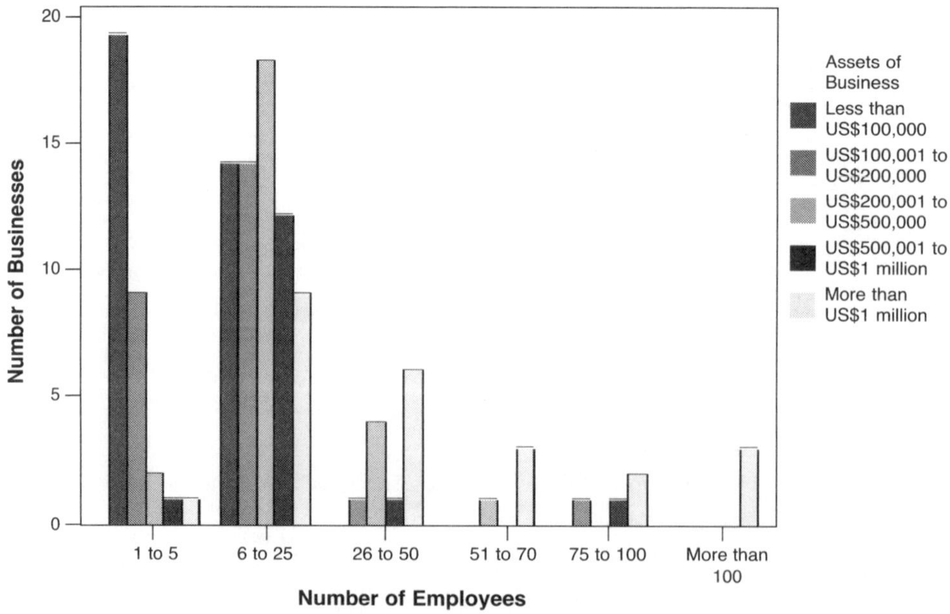

expectation that the services sector accounts for the majority of SMEs, while hospitality and distribution are also popular areas of economic activity for SMEs in the Caribbean.

Figure 1.4: Distribution of Businesses by Product Type

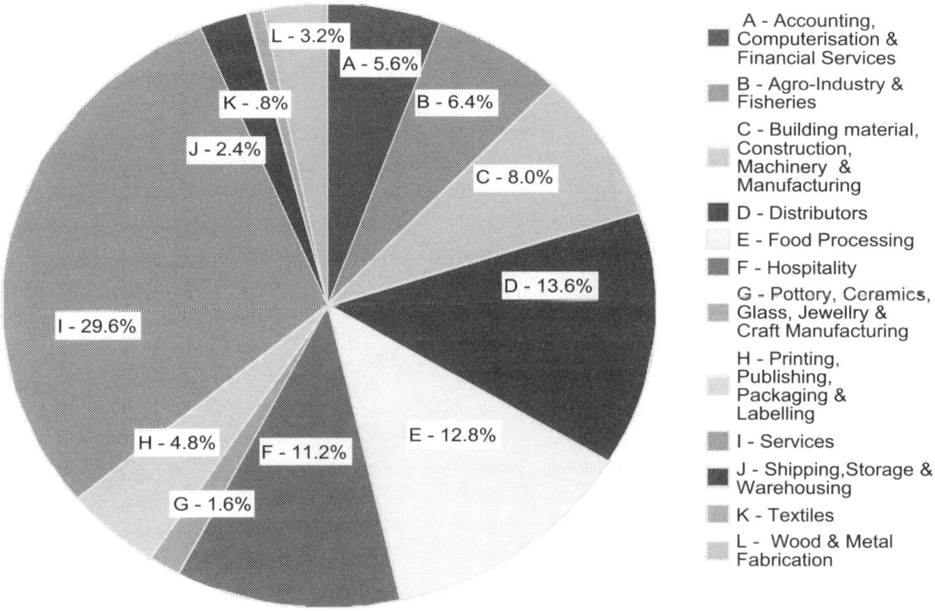

Distribution of Businesses by Country and Legal Form

The businesses selected for sampling were drawn from ten CARICOM countries, although they are not spread evenly over the countries (Figure 1.5). This was because of the relative difficulty encountered in various countries in securing the participation of businesses. The reasons for this varied from security concerns to the parochial and secretive nature of some owners, who refuse to reveal their 'private business'. A more even country distribution was not possible given the time constraints within which the survey was conducted.

Figure 1.6 shows that privately incorporated businesses form the largest section of businesses by legal form (61.3%), with sole proprietorships accounting for 28.2 per cent of businesses. This may indicate the relative ease of incorporation in most countries, rather than legal sophistication among entrepreneurs.

The majority of businesses appear to be more than ten years old. Figure 1.7 shows that most enterprises (27.8%) had been operating for between ten and 19 years, with a further 23.7 per cent in business for 20 years or more. Start-ups, that is, businesses in existence for less than three years, constituted 15 per cent of the total number of businesses surveyed. Businesses which had been in operation for up to five years account for 25.6 per cent of the total. This would seem to indicate that new businesses are not growing very rapidly as yet, and that there is a great deal of room for a higher rate of growth.

Figure 1.5: Distribution of Businesses by Country

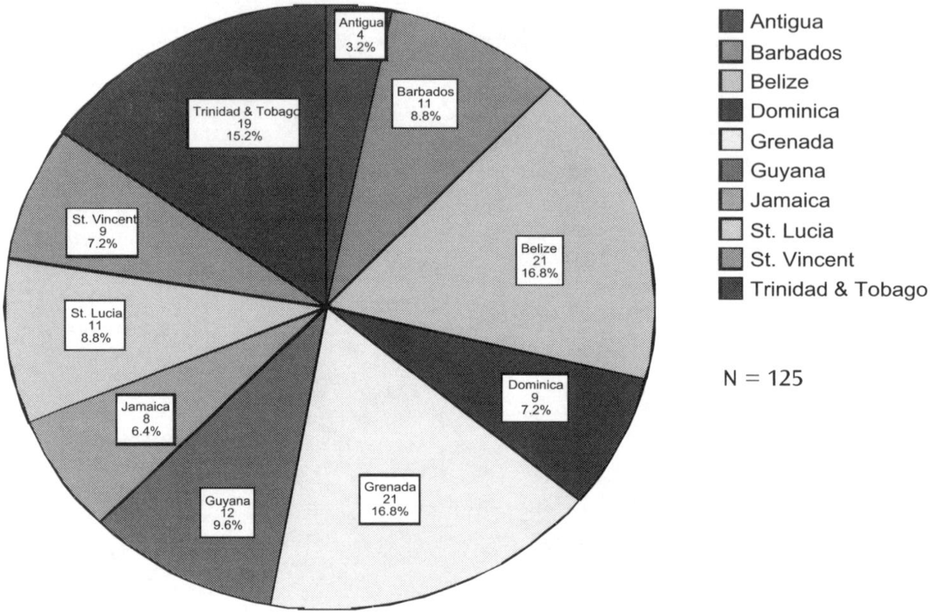

Figure 1.6: Distribution of Businesses by Legal Form

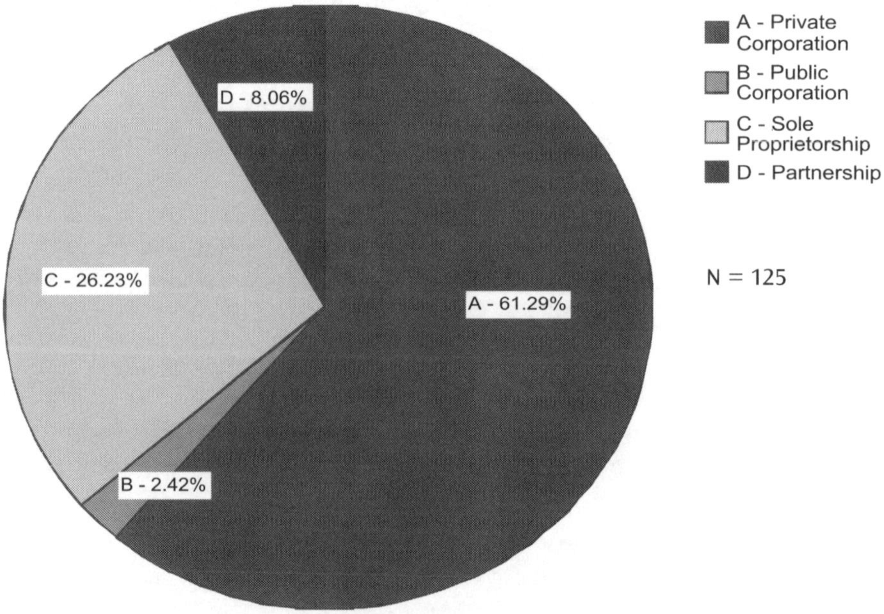

Figure 1.7: Distribution of Businesses by Years in Business

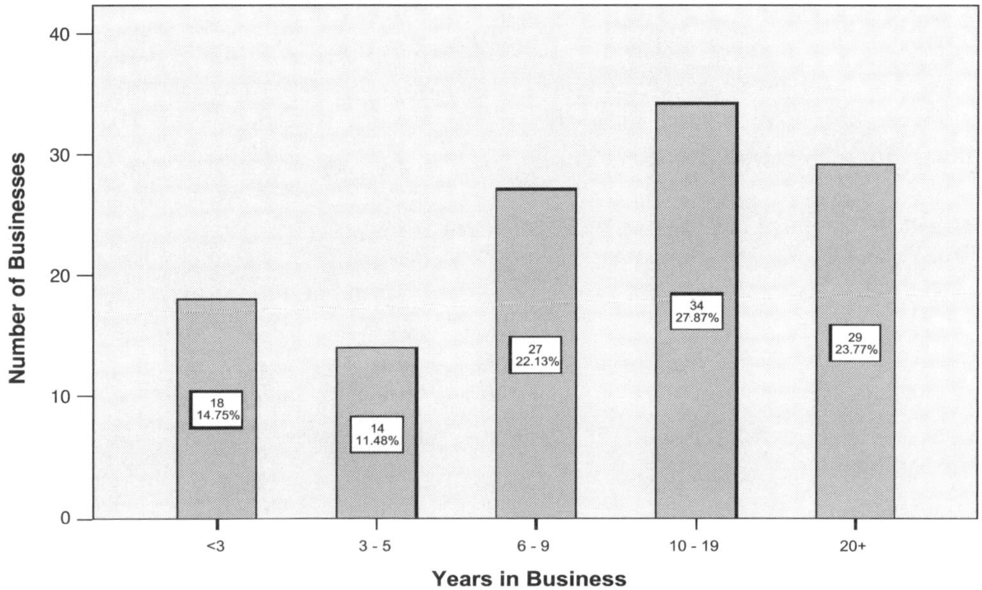

When examined in relation to the number of employees (see Table A1.4 of Appendix 2), this figures does not significantly improve: only 22 per cent of all businesses with between six and 25 employees were in existence for up to five years. Figure 1.8 shows the distribution by years in business. As is to be expected, most of the smaller businesses – with fewer than six employees – had been in business for between one and nine years, while businesses with a larger numbers of employees had been in existence for longer periods.

Figure 1.8: Distribution of Businesses (Number of Employees) by Years in Business

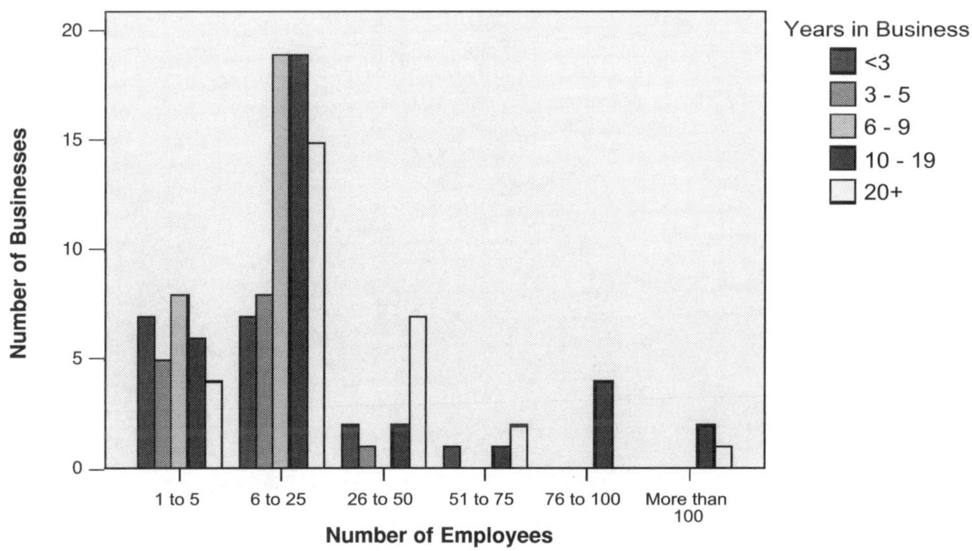

Original Base of Businesses

Most SMEs (88%), as shown in Figure 1.9, were started from scratch, and more than 53 per cent were originally based in the homes of their owners. This suggests that the majority of these businesses had to rely on their own resources at start-up. It also indicates a fair degree of entrepreneurialism on the part of the current owners. Table 1.1 shows the origins of the businesses by legal form.

Table 1.1: Origin of Businesses by Legal Form

		Origin of business				
		Started from scratch	Purchased an existing business	Took over family business	Spin-off from another business	Total
Type of business						
Partnership	Number	8	1	1	0	10
	Percentage of type of business	80.0	10.0	10.0	0.0	100.0
Sole proprietorship	Number	31	0	4	0	35
	Percentage of type of business	88.6	0.0	11.4	0.0	100.0
Public corporation	Number	3	0	0	0	3
	Percentage of type of business	100.0	0.0	0.0	0.0	100.0
Private corporation	Number	67	4	4	1	76
	Percentage of type of business	88.2	5.3	5.3	1.3	100.0
Total	Number	109	5	9	1	124
	Percentage	87.9	4.0	7.3	0.8	100.0

Figure 1.9: Distribution of Businesses by Origin of Business

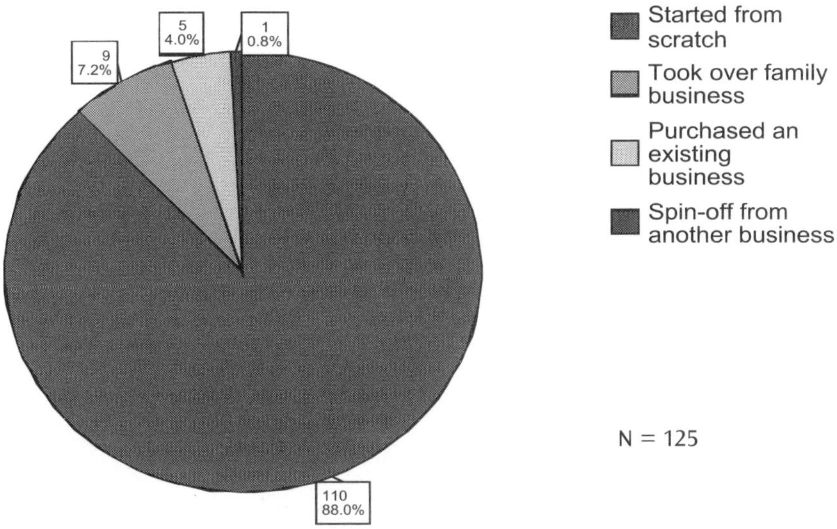

Exports and Areas to which Products Were Exported

Forty-two (34.7%) of the businesses that responded reported that they exported some portion of their product or service. Of these, 39 indicated the destinations of their exports. Of these 39 businesses, the majority exported to CARICOM countries (35.7%), followed by the USA and Canada (18.4%) and other Caribbean countries (14.3%).

Table 1.2: Areas to which Products Were Exported and Mean Percentages of Total Product

	N		Mean %
	Valid	Percentage	
CARICOM	35	35.7	56.83
Other Caribbean countries	14	14.3	8.07
Central/South America	9	9.1	17.78
Europe	13	13.3	21.85
USA and Canada	18	18.4	26.39
Asia	4	4.1	3.25
Other	5	5.1	5.00

Principal Owner Characteristics

Figure 1.10: Distribution of Businesses by Gender of Majority Owner

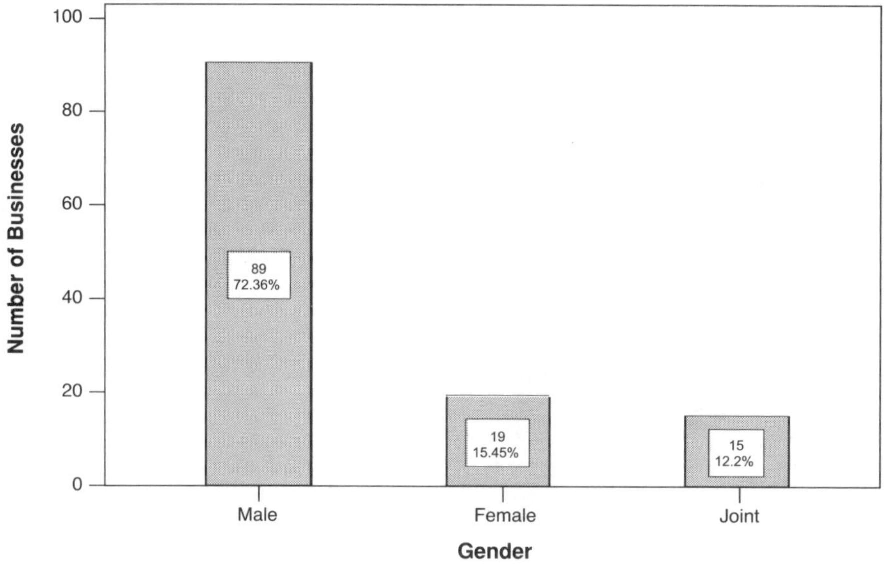

A minority of SMEs, accounting for 15 per cent of the total number of businesses surveyed, were owned by women. If businesses with joint male and female ownership are included, women had an ownership share in 27.2 per cent of the businesses surveyed.

Figure 1.11: Distribution of Businesses by Age of Majority Owner

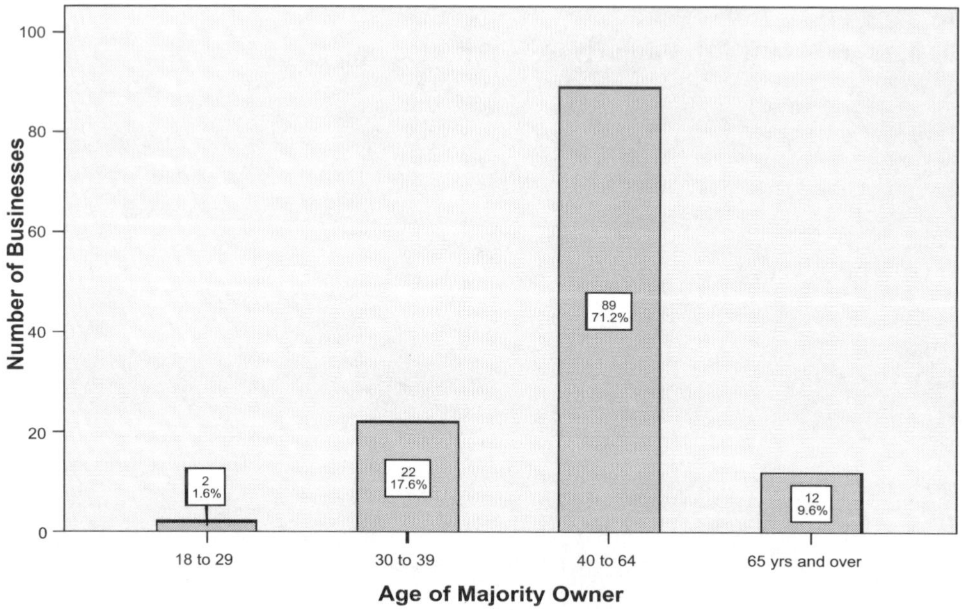

The majority of businesses (89%) were owned by people between the ages of 30 to 64. Only two businesses were owned by people aged between 18 and 29 years old.

Figure 1.12 Distribution of Businesses by Educational Level of Majority Owner

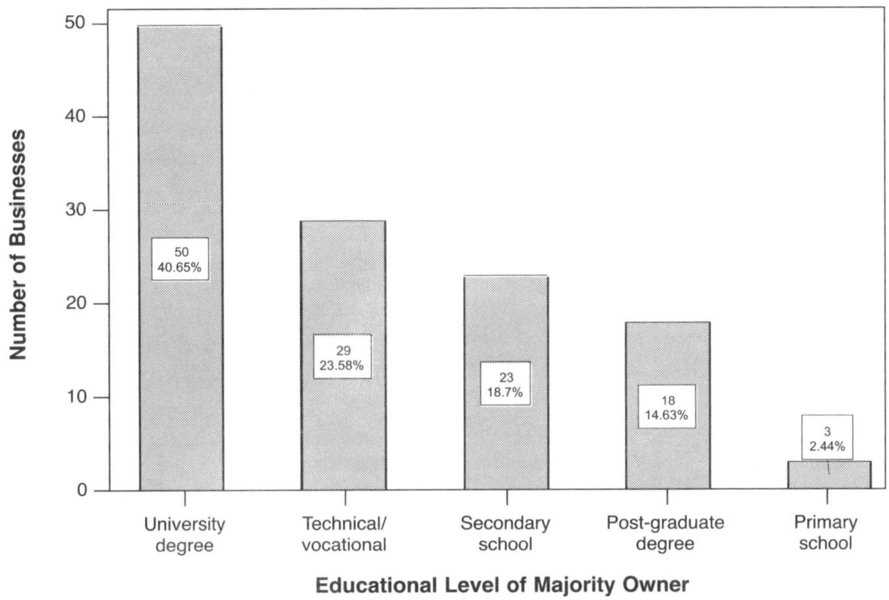

Fifty-six per cent of owners claimed to have university degrees. This is a reasonably high figure for SME ownership and reflects the relatively high level of education in the CARICOM countries as a whole.

As the majority of owners were aged between 30 and 64 years, it is not surprising that the experience of the majority of owners reflected their ages. Sixty-four per cent of owners had 16 years or more experience in their businesses. This number rose to 81 per cent for an experience level of more than eight years. These results are shown in Figure 1.13.

The self-assessment of owners of their ability to cope with several aspects of management appears from the responses to be generally high. Asked to rate their experience on several measures on a scale of 1 to5, with 1 being 'little or no experience' and 5 being 'very experienced', the mean score on all levels was just under 4. The 'whiskers' below and above the boxes in Figure 1.14 indicate the lowest and highest scores on each scale.

Table A1.6 of Appendix 2 tabulates the responses to the question about managerial skills possessed by SMEs. Table A1.7 of Appendix 2 shows the self-professed experience of the managements of SMEs by gender, for start-ups (less than three years in business) and for rapid growth rate businesses.

Figure 1.13: Distribution of Businesses by Number of Years Experience of Majority Owner

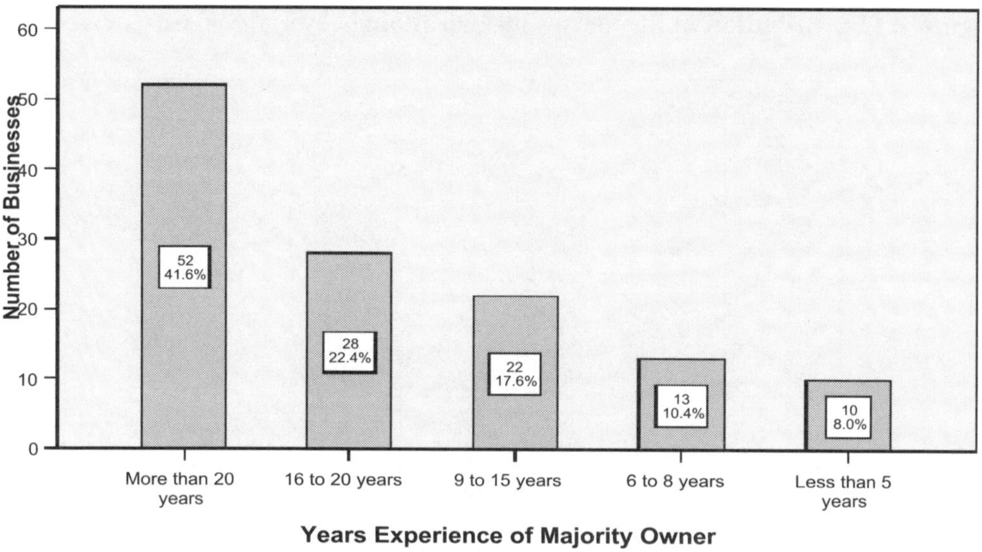

Figure 1.14: Owners' Self-confidence in Their Own Abilities

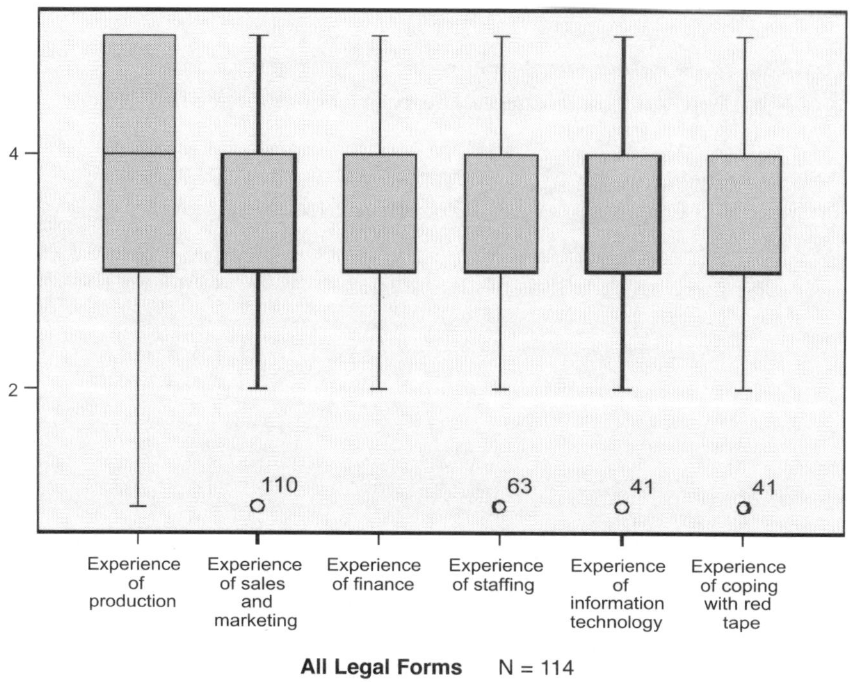

As can be seen below, with 65 per cent of 123 respondents acknowledging that they had never sought support from a business service provider, this self-confidence does not seem misplaced. Those who sought advice did so mostly during the process of setting up the company (11.2%) and when the company started to grow (11.2%).

II Attempts by SMEs to Access Finance

Part II explores the responses actually recorded by SMEs in relation to their experience in accessing long-term and other forms of finance, and the impact of that experience. The survey inquired into the requests made for debt finance, equity finance and grant finance or facilitation. It also explored the extent to which such requests were approved or turned down by lenders or terminated by the borrower, and why the latter failed to meet the conditions required by the lender.

The extent to which SMEs maintained long-term relationships with credit providers was examined, in order to ascertain whether this had a facilitating effect. The extent to which SMEs were satisfied with the non-cost elements of banking services was explored, as well as the most frequently accessed lending institution.

With regard to equity finance, the source from which such finance was sought was examined, together with the success rate. Government grants were also looked at and the result of such requests noted.

The following are the results of these inquiries.

2

Requests for Debt Finance

When examined by number of employees, the results show that of 124 businesses that responded, 78 (62.9%) had requested some form of finance. Table 2.1 shows that the larger businesses were proportionately more likely to request finance than the smaller businesses. When analysed by years in business (see Table 2.2), the results show that 76 businesses reported having requested finance, with businesses more than six years old being more likely to have done so.

Table 2.1: Requests for Finance in Last Three Years by Number of Employees

Number of employees	Number in sample	Percentage of sample	Request for finance in last three years	Percentage of sample
Over 100	3	2.4	2	66.7
76–100	4	3.2	4	100.0
51–75	4	3.2	4	100.0
26–50	12	9.7	8	66.7
6–25	69	55.6	43	62.3
1–5	32	25.8	17	53.1
Total	124	100.0	78	62.9

An attempt to analyse the request rates for businesses of differing sizes was made with the following result. Proportionately, businesses with greater assets were more likely to request finance than smaller businesses. Table A2.1 of Appendix 2 shows that more than 80 per cent of businesses with assets of over US$500,000 had made requests for finance, compared with 59 per cent of businesses with assets of under US$100,000. Table A2.2 of Appendix 2 shows that the rate of growth also seems to have some bearing on requests for debt finance, as businesses which grew rapidly and moderately well tended to request debt finance more than those whose growth was slower. As Table A2.3 of Appendix 2 shows, private companies made more requests for finance, followed by sole proprietorships; this was to be expected as these two forms of enterprise were the predominant forms of ownership.

Table 2.2: Requests for Finance in Last Three Years by Years in Business

		Request for finance in last three years		
		Yes	No	Total
Years in business				
20+	Number	19	10	29
	Percentage of group	65.5	34.5	100.0
10–19	Number	22	12	34
	Percentage of group	64.7	35.3	100.0
6–9	Number	19	8	27
	Percentage of group	70.4	29.6	100.0
3–5	Number	7	7	14
	Percentage of group	50.0	50.0	100.0
<3	Number	9	9	18
	Percentage of group	50.0	50.0	100.0
Total	Number	76	46	122
	Percentage	62.3	37.7	100.0

Type of Finance Requested

Table 2.3: Type of Finance Requested

	Responses		Percentage of cases
	N	Percentage	
Type of finance requested			
Demand	34	29.8	44.7
Long-term loan	28	24.6	36.8
Mortgage loan	16	14.0	21.1
Increase in line of credit limit	12	10.5	15.8
New line of credit	11	9.6	14.5
New credit card	7	6.1	9.2
Increase credit card limit	2	1.8	2.6
Other	4	3.5	5.3
Total	114	100.0	

Short-term loans, as shown in Table 2.3, are the most frequently requested loans, followed closely by long-term loans. However, when mortgage loans are added to other long-term loans, these become the most frequently requested type of finance. Table A2.4 of Appendix 2 shows the types of finance requested in the last three years by type of business. Figure A2.5 of Appendix 2 shows the percentage of businesses by number of employees requesting various types of finance.

Figure 2.1 and Table A2.6 of Appendix 2 show the percentage of businesses by revenue size that requested various forms of finance as follows:

1. Demand loans were more frequently requested than any other type of loan by all businesses except for businesses of between US$500,000 and US$1 million, where the most frequent request was for long-term loans;
2. Demand loans were more frequently requested by businesses with a revenue of between US$100,000 and US$200,000;
3. Long-term loans were more frequently requested by larger businesses with a revenue of over US$500,000;
4. Only the larger businesses were interested in increases in lines of credit;
5. Mortgage loans and long-term loans were the second most frequently requested form of loan for all sizes of business.

Figure 2.1: Percentage of Businesses Requesting Various Types of Financial Products by Revenue

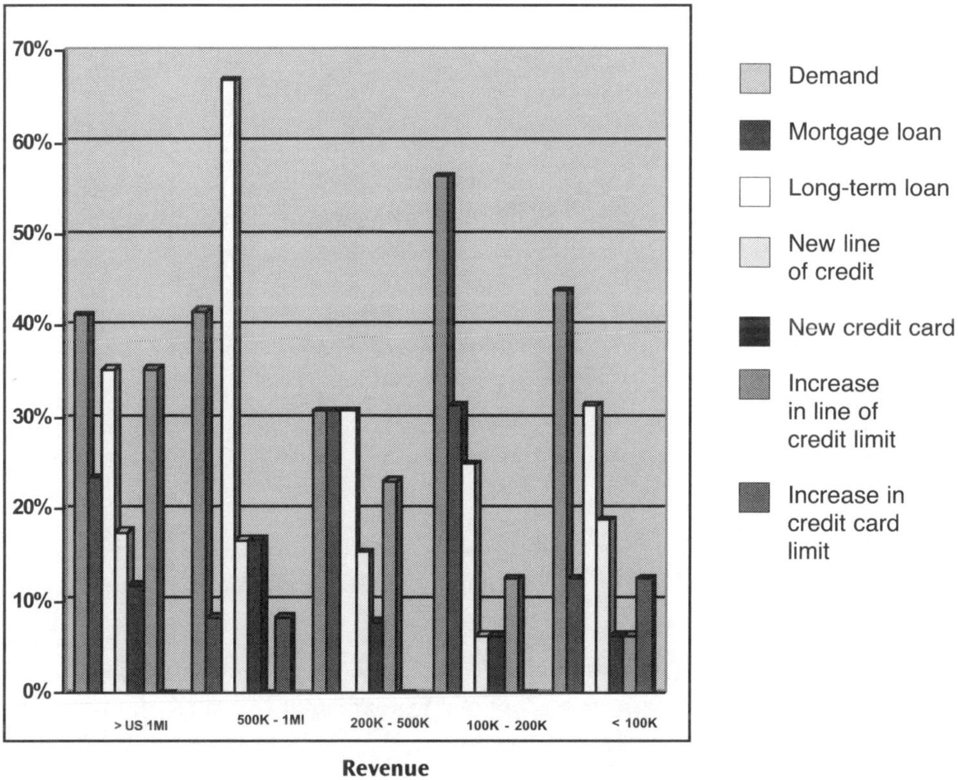

Lending Institutions Approached

Of the lending institutions approached for finance, banks were by far the most frequently used, as shown in Table 2.4. Eight-seven per cent of all requests for debt finance were made to banks, with credit unions accounting for 6.5 per cent of requests. This is not surprising, as banks are generally seen as the main providers of finance for almost all purposes. However, this result highlights the fact that institutions such as trust companies and insurance companies do not appear to be in the market as providers of finance to SMEs.

Table 2.4: Types of Financial Institution to which Requests Were Made for Finance

		Frequency	Percentage	Valid percentage	Cumulative percentage
Valid	Commercial bank	67	53.6	87.0	87.0
	Credit union	5	4.0	6.5	93.5
	Other financial institution	3	2.4	3.9	97.4
	Government agency	2	1.6	2.6	100.0
	Total	77	61.6	100.0	
Missing	System	48	38.4		
Total		125	100.0		

Authorisation of Debt Finance

Finance was authorised in the case of 51 (69.9%) of the 73 businesses which applied for it. This represents 40.8 per cent of the total sample. Table 2.5 shows authorisation of finance to businesses broken down by number of employees. Table A2.7 of Appendix 2 shows the number of businesses that requested and had finance authorised in the last three years by business characteristics. The table shows that:

1. Businesses with between six and 25 employees were proportionately most successful, followed by businesses with between 26 and 50 employees;
2. Businesses with a turnover of between US$200,000 and US$500,000 were the most successful, followed by those with a turnover of between US$100,000 and US$200,000;
3. The sectors that were proportionately the most successful were: (a) printing and publishing, packaging and labelling; (b) shipping, storage and warehousing; and (c) wood and metal manufacturing;
4. Businesses in Guyana, Trinidad and Tobago, and Belize were more likely to have finance authorised than those in other countries: requests in Antigua, Dominica and Grenada were least likely to be successful;
5. Applications by businesses with joint male and female ownership were proportionately most successful, followed by applications by male-owned businesses.

Table 2.5: Businesses for which Finance was Authorised by Number of Employees

		Authorisation of credit		
		Yes	No	Total
Number of employees				
More than 100	Number	1	1	2
	Percentage of group	2.0	4.5	2.7
76–100	Number	2	2	4
	Percentage of group	3.9	9.1	5.5
51–75	Number	3	1	4
	Percentage of group	5.9	4.5	5.5
26–50	Number	7	2	9
	Percentage of group	13.7	9.1	12.3
6–25	Number	32	8	40
	Percentage of group	62.7	36.4	54.8
1 to 5	Number	6	8	14
	Percentage of group	11.8	36.4	19.2
Total	Number	51	22	73
	Percentage	100.0	100.0	100.0

Proportionately, the larger businesses were more successful in having their requests authorised. Fifty-three per cent of businesses with assets of under US$100,000 had their requests for finance authorised, compared with 67 per cent of businesses with assets of over US$500,000 (see Table A2.8 of Appendix 2). However, 91 per cent of businesses with assets of between US$200,001 and US$500,000 also had their requests approved.

Amounts Authorised and Borrowed

Table 2.6: Amount of Finance Authorised (US Currency Equivalent)

	Demand or short-term	Mortgage loan	Long-term loan	New line of credit	New credit card	Increase in line of credit	Increase in credit card limit
N Valid	25	6	5	0	2	2	0
Missing	100	119	120	125	123	123	125
Mean	$118,000	$486,000	$279,200		$21,250	$101,500	
Mode	$125,000[a]	$2,500,000[a]	$500,000		$37,500[a]	$200,000[a]	
Minimum	$3,000	$5,000	$121,000		$5,000.	$3,000	
Maximum	$1,100,000	$2,500,000	$500,000		$37,500	$200,000	
Sum	$2,950,000	$2,916,000	$1,396,000		$42,500	$203,000	

[a]Multiple modes exist. The smallest value is shown.

Table 2.7: Amount of Finance Actually Borrowed (US Currency Equivalent)

	Demand or short-term loan[a]	Mortgage loan[a]	Long-term loan[a]	New line of credit[a]	New credit card[a]	Increase in line of credit[a]	Increase in credit card limit[a]
N Valid	21	4	4	0	1	1	0
Missing	104	121	121	125	124	124	125
Mean	$123,714	$81,000	$536,500		$2,500	$200,000	
Mode	$54,000[b]	$150,000[b]	$1,400,000[b]		$2,500	$200,000	
Minimum	$3,000	$5,000	$121,000		$2,500	$200,000	
Maximum	$1,100,000	$150,000	$1,400,000		$2,500	$200,000	
Sum	$2,598,000	$324,000	$2,146,000		$2,500	$200,000	

[a]Local currency
[b]Multiple modes exist. The smallest value is shown.

It was not possible to obtain detailed information on actual amounts approved and borrowed for the entire sample. For reasons of confidentiality, security or just plain secretiveness many SMEs declined to provide this information even if they admitted to having had finance authorised and actually having borrowed some amounts. However, 40 (78.4%) of the businesses that had had some credit approved provided information on the amount of finance authorised, while 31 (60.7%) provided information on actual amounts borrowed. This information is tabulated in Tables 2.6 and 2.7. It will be seen from Table 2.6 that the majority of loans approved were demand or short-term loans. Of 25 short-term loans authorised, the mean amount was US$118,000. Five long-term loans were authorised with a mean value of US$279,200. However, when these authorisations are added to mortgage loans this number rises to 11, with total approvals of US$4.3 million. Information on amounts actually borrowed was even scarcer, again because of the reticence of SMEs to disclose these sums. Table 2.7 shows that 21 demand or short-term loans were actually taken out, with a mean value of US$123,714. Four mortgage loans and four long-term loans were also taken out, with a total value of US$2,470,000. The discrepancy between authorised long-term loans and sums actually borrowed is accounted for by one respondent who indicated that a foreign currency loan was authorised, but a local currency loan actually taken. Because of the incompleteness and variability of the responses these figures are not sufficiently accurate to be meaningful. They are, however, probably representative of the kinds of amounts requested and authorised for SMEs on average.

Rejection Rate

As we have seen, requests for debt finance were unsuccessful in 31 per cent of the cases where credit was requested. Table 2.8 shows that only 18 SMEs provided the reasons why finance was declined. Of these, the commonest reasons reported by SMEs were insufficient cash flow, insufficient collateral, insufficient equity, insufficient information and management inexperience. 'Other' reasons were that the credit supplier did not wish to take the risk or thought that lending to the business was too high a risk.

Table 2.8: Reasons for Declining to Provide the Amount of Finance Requested

	Responses		Percentage of cases
	N	Percentage	
Reasons for refusal of finance			
Insufficient cash flow	2	11.1	28.6
Insufficient collateral	2	11.1	28.6
Insufficient equity	2	11.1	28.6
Insufficient information	2	11.1	28.6
Management team inexperienced	2	11.1	28.6
Insufficient income	1	5.6	14.3
Insufficient working capital	1	5.6	14.3
Poor credit experience or history	1	5.6	14.3
Business plan not acceptable	1	5.6	14.3
Would not personally guarantee	1	5.6	14.3
Other	3	16.7	42.9
Total	18	100.0	

Authorisation and rejection rates by country are shown in Table A 2.9 of Appendix 2. Both requests for finance and the authorisation rates correlate with the educational level of the majority owners; as the majority of owners possessed university degrees, this is not surprising. These results are shown in Tables A2.10 and A 2.11 of Appendix 2.

Relationship with Lending Institutions

Table 2.9: Authorisation of Credit by Length of Time Doing Business with Financial Institution

	Authorisation of credit		
	Yes	No	Total
Length of time doing business with financial institution			
0–5 years	4	6	10
6–10 years	10	4	14
Over 10 years	25	6	31
Total	39	16	55

The length of time enterprises had been banking with the financial institution from which they sought finance seems to be positively correlated with approval of the request. Table 2.9 shows that the longer the period of time the enterprise had been doing business with the financial institution, the greater the number of authorisations of requests.

This is consistent with the finding that the majority of enterprises had been in business for more than nine years. As Table A2.12 of Appendix 2 shows, the longer the enterprise had been in business, the greater the likelihood that credit would be approved.

Satisfaction with the Service Elements of Financial Institutions

Only enterprises which had made requests for finance were asked how satisfied they were with the non-cost services provided by financial institutions. Satisfaction was tested on five levels: availability of finance; range of services; competence of staff; efficiency of service; and understanding of customers' business needs. Table A2.13 of Appendix 2 shows that on all levels except 'availability of finance', between 25 per cent and 32 per cent of all respondents claimed to be 'somewhat dissatisfied' with these services. Only 35.1 per cent of respondents declared themselves to be 'very satisfied' with the availability of finance. Table A2.14 of Appendix 2 shows that satisfaction with the services of financial institutions increased with the length of time the enterprises had been doing business with them.

Discouragement of Finance

Table 2.10 shows that of the businesses surveyed, 43 (34.4%) did not attempt to obtain finance: 48.8 per cent of these did not need finance, while 20.9 per cent thought the application process was too difficult and 16.3 per cent thought that the cost of debt finance was too high. The last two issues appear to be the main factors which discouraged businesses from applying for finance. The businesses that did not need finance represent 16.7 per cent of the total sample, indicating that it is possible that some SMEs were not interested in further expansion and were content to manage their businesses in their current state. This is a subject for further examination.

Table 2.10: Reasons Why Businesses Did Not Attempt to Obtain Finance

		Frequency	Percentage	Valid percentage	Cumulative percentage
Valid	Finance not needed	21	16.8	48.8	48.8
	Applying for finance too difficult	9	7.2	20.9	69.8
	Cost of debt finance too high	7	5.6	16.3	86.0
	Do not like to be in debt	3	2.4	7.0	93.0
	Other	2	1.6	4.7	97.7
	Thought request would be turned down	1	.8	2.3	100.0
	Total	43	34.4	100.0	
Missing	System	82	65.6		
Total		125	100.0		

Table A.2.15 of Appendix 2 shows the breakdown by business characteristics in numbers and percentages for businesses that did not need finance.

Intended Use of Finance

Table 2.11: Intended Use of Finance

	Responses		Percentage of cases
	N	Percentage	
Intended use of finance			
To buy machinery and equipment	36	16.9	45.6
Inventory financing	35	16.4	44.3
Working capital	31	14.6	39.2
To buy buildings and land	26	12.2	32.9
To buy vehicles	23	10.8	29.1
Product and service development	20	9.4	25.3
Research and development	14	6.6	17.7
Debt collection	14	6.6	17.7
Accounts receivable	5	2.3	6.3
Business acquisition	4	1.9	5.1
Export financing	3	1.4	3.8
Other	2	0.9	2.5
Total	213	100.0	

Table 2.11 shows the main uses for which finance was wanted. These include, in order of priority, the purchase of machinery and equipment, inventory financing, working capital and the purchase of buildings and land, and of vehicles. This is true of all businesses, whether they are broken down by number of employees, assets or years in business.

Collateral

Respondents were more willing to disclose whether collateral was requested in their attempts to seek finance, than to disclose the actual amounts authorised and borrowed. Of 64 respondents who answered this question, 66 per cent said that they were required to provide guarantees of personal assets, while 58 per cent were required to provide guarantees on the assets of the business. Tables 2.12 and 2.13 indicate that in the majority of cases financial institutions seek some form of guarantee for loans authorised.

Table 2.12: Were Personal Assets Requested as Collateral?

		Frequency	Percentage	Valid percentage	Cumulative percentage
Valid	Yes	42	33.6	65.6	65.6
	No	22	17.6	34.4	100.0
	Total	64	51.2	100.0	
Missing	System	61	48.8		
Total		125	100.0		

Table 2.13: Were Business Assets Requested as Collateral?

		Frequency	Percentage	Valid percentage	Cumulative percentage
Valid	Yes	34	27.2	57.6	57.6
	No	25	20.0	42.4	100.0
	Total	59	47.2	100.0	
Missing	System	66	52.8		
Total		125	100.0		

The Application Process

Sixty-four of the respondents specified the documents that were requested as part of the application process. Apart from the formal application for finance, the most frequently requested documents were business financial statements, cash flow projections and a business plan. Personal financial statements and an appraisal of assets to be financed were also requested in 42 per cent of cases. These results are shown in Table 2.14. Eighty per cent had no difficulty in completing the application process. As shown in Table 2.15, of the 20 per cent who experienced some difficulties, the most frequent complaints related to the amount of information requested, the difficulties in obtaining the information and the need for further explanation of the terms and conditions.

Table 2.14: Documents Requested

N = 64

	Responses		Percentage of cases
	N	Percentage	
Documents requested as part of the application process			
Business financial statements	46	16.8	71.9
Formal application for finance	45	16.5	70.3
Cash flow projections	34	12.5	53.1
Business plan	34	12.5	53.1
Audited business financial statements	33	12.1	51.6
Personal financial statements	27	9.9	42.2
Appraisals of assets to be financed	27	9.9	42.2
Feasibility study	13	4.8	20.3
References from business personnel	4	1.5	6.3
Franchise agreement	2	0.7	3.1
Other documentation	6	2.2	9.4
No document requested	2	0.7	3.1
Total	273	100.0	

Table 2.15: Difficulties Encountered in Completing the Application Process

	Responses		Percentage of cases
	N	Percentage	
Difficulties with application process			
Too much information required	10	55.6	83.3
Needed further explanation of terms and conditions	2	11.1	16.7
Could not obtain information required	2	11.1	16.7
Could not provide a business plan or future projections	1	5.6	8.3
Did not have any accounting records	1	5.6	8.3
Other	2	11.1	16.7
Total	18	100.0	

In general, SMEs are not reluctant to make requests for debt finance. As we have seen, 63 per cent of all businesses surveyed by employee size made requests for debt finance. Of these, 69.9 per cent had their applications approved. However, of the total number of businesses surveyed, only 44 per cent had their applications approved.

3

Requests for Equity Finance

Figure 3.1 shows that 17 enterprises, or 13.6 per cent of the total surveyed, sought equity finance. Fourteen (82.4%) of those seeking equity finance were successful. Table A3.1 of Appendix 2 shows that equity finance was provided by a friend or relative in 53 per cent of cases; this was by far the most prevalent source of equity finance.

Table A3.2 of Appendix 2 shows that the likelihood of obtaining equity finance correlated with asset size. The larger the assets of a business, the more likely it was to be able to obtain equity finance.

Figure 3.1: Requests for Equity Finance

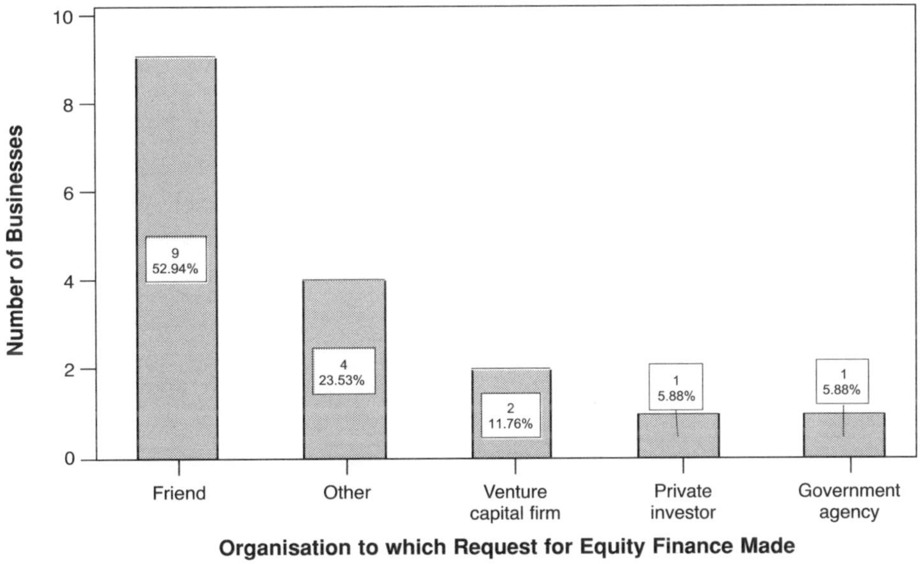

4

Requests for Grants

Table 4.1 shows that only 19 (14.5%) of businesses pursued government grants. This is possibly because there is a perception that such assistance is not available, notwithstanding all the efforts of governments in this direction.

Table 4.1: Request for Government Grant

		Frequency	Percentage	Valid percentage	Cumulative percentage
Valid	Yes	18	14.4	14.5	14.5
	No	106	84.8	85.5	100.0
	Total	124	99.2	100.0	
Missing	System	1	.8		
Total		125	100.0		

Table 4.2 indicates that seven (36.8%) of the 19 businesses which requested some form of grant or subsidy were successful in obtaining it. As Table A4.1 of Appendix 2 shows, the success rate does not appear to be correlated with the asset size of the business.

Table 4.2: Was Grant or Subsidy Finance Obtained?

		Frequency	Percentage	Valid percentage	Cumulative percentage
Valid	No	12	9.6	63.2	63.2
	Yes	7	5.6	36.8	100.0
	Total	19	15.2	100.0	
Missing	System	106	84.8		
Total		125	100.0		

III Perceptions of SMEs on Access to Finance and Inhibitors to Access

5

The Finance Needs of Businesses

Figure 5.1 demonstrates that 22.1 per cent of respondents thought that a sum of between US$100,001 and US$250,000 would be the maximum financing need of their business if it could be obtained on reasonable terms and conditions. 19.7 per cent, however, required between US$25,000 and US$50,000. Altogether, 45.9 per cent required less than US$100,000.

Figure 5.1: Maximum Finance Needs of Businesses

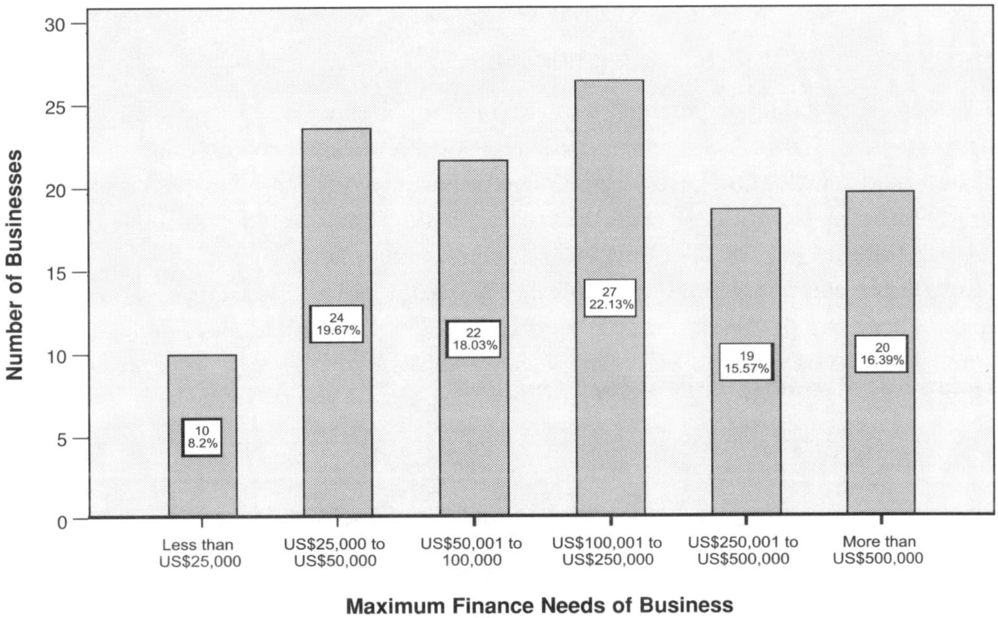

Figure 5.2 shows that the larger businesses by assets required larger amounts of finance. However, seven businesses with assets of less than US$100,000 required between US$50,000 and US$100,000, and another seven with assets of between US$100,000 and US$200,000 required finance of US$100,000 and US$250,000. This appears to indicate that these smaller businesses still felt sufficiently confident to assume debt of fairly large amounts in order to expand their enterprises.

Figure 5.2: Maximum Finance Needs of Businesses by Asset Size

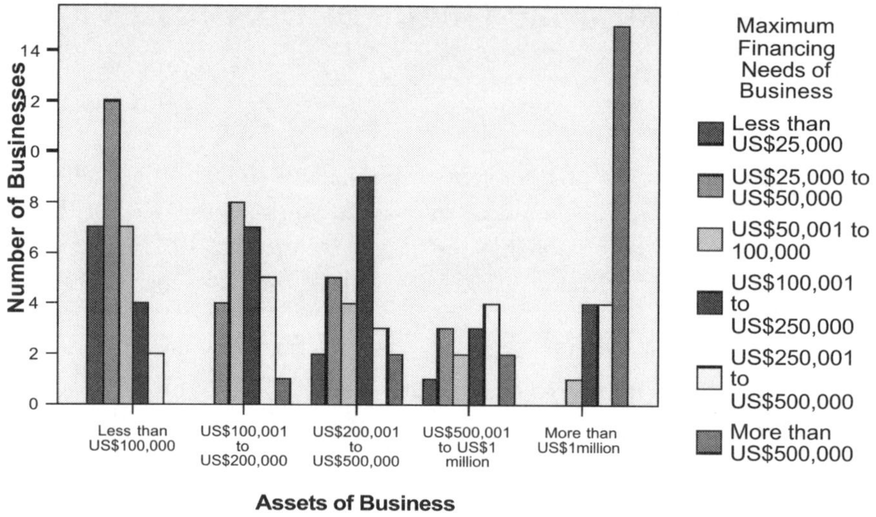

Figure 5.3 shows that the maximum financing term required by 85.3 per cent of respondents was ten years or less. For 47.5 per cent of the respondents, a period of up to six years would suffice. The largest percentage of businesses (27%) expressed a preference for loans for periods of nine or ten years, suggesting that a significant number of them regarded this as 'long term'. Only 14.7 per cent required a loan for a period of over ten years. This seems to suggest that long-term finance for periods over ten years is not a very high priority among SMEs, and that on the whole they prefer periods of under ten years.

Figure 5.3: Maximum Term of Loan Required

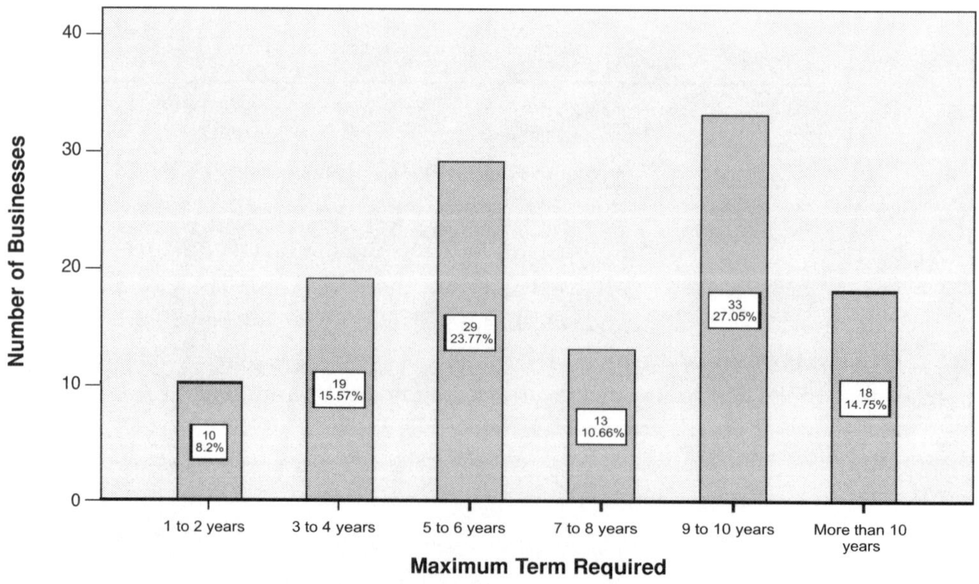

Employees and Revenues Businesses Would Add in the Next Five Years

The respondents were asked how many employees they would add to their operations over the next five years if they could secure finance to develop their businesses. They were also asked approximately how much additional revenue per annum could be generated by their businesses in similar circumstances. One hundred and fifteen respondents estimated they could add a total of 1,233 employees over the next five years, with the modal number being five and the mean 11. In answer to the second question, 105 respondents thought they could add a total of just over US$25 million per annum in revenue if finance were available. It is difficult to assess these responses. The commitment to add employees seems small compared with the optimistic assessment of the revenue that would be added. Table 5.1 shows the responses to these questions.

Table 5.1: Employees and Revenue that Would Be Added

Employees

N	Valid	115
	Missing	10
Mean		10.72
Mode		5
Total		1233

Number of employees who would be added over the next five years

Revenue

N	Valid	105
	Missing	20
Mean		$241,661.90
Mode		$50,000
Total		$25,374,500

Revenue that would be added per annum

Purposes for which Finance Would be Used

Businesses were asked to what purpose finance would be put if it could be secured. Table 5.2 indicates that the main use of finance would be to purchase machinery and equipment, followed by product and service development and inventory financing. The purchase of land and buildings was the fourth priority, indicating that long-term finance for that purpose is not a major need for SMEs. It is also possible that they do not have a perception of their businesses on a larger scale or are daunted by the prospect of undertaking greater debt. These issues are worth further examination.

Table 5.2: Purpose for which Finance Would Be Used

N = 121

	Responses		Percentage of cases
	N	Percentage	
Purpose of application for finance			
To buy machinery and equipment	73	20.5	60.3
Product and service development	69	19.4	57.0
Inventory financing	56	15.7	46.3
Building and land acquisition	49	13.8	40.5
Research and development	39	11.0	32.2
To buy vehicles	35	9.8	28.9
Debt consolidation	32	9.0	26.4
Business acquisition	3	0.8	2.5
Total	356	100.0	

Support for SMEs and Obstacles to Development

The organisations that are seen as providing the most support for SMEs are banks and credit unions, with the former having a convincing lead. International donors are more favourably regarded than local government agencies or national governments. As can be seen from Tables A5.1 and A5.2 of Appendix 2, these rankings do not change depending on the number of employees or assets of the business.

Table 5.3: Organisations Providing the Most Support for SMEs

N = 115

	Responses		Percentage of cases
	N	Percentage	
Organisations providing most support			
Banks	70	34.5	60.9
Credit unions	55	27.1	47.8
International donors	25	12.3	21.7
Local government agencies	17	8.4	14.8
Consulting companies and agencies	13	6.4	11.3
National government	13	6.4	11.3
Large foreign enterprises	3	1.5	2.6
Service centres	2	1.0	1.7
Large state enterprises	1	.5	.9
Other organisation	4	2.0	3.5
Total	203	100.0	

Main Causes of Difficulty in Securing Long-term Finance

Respondents were asked to rate in order of priority the main reasons why businesses find it difficult to secure long-term finance. Table 5.4 shows that the main difficulties in securing long-term finance in the view of SMEs are insufficient collateral and an inadequate income from the business. These are the same causes noted by a much smaller group of SMEs in Table 2.8 as the reasons offered by lending institutions for refusing to provide requested finance.

Table 5.4: Main Causes of Difficulty in Securing Long-term Finance

	Responses		Percentage of cases
	N	Percentage	
Causes of difficulties in securing long-term finance			
Insufficient collateral	32	28.6	28.6
Insufficient income or revenue	28	25.0	25.0
Insufficient cash flow	11	9.8	9.8
Insufficient working capital	10	8.9	8.9
Insufficient equity	7	6.3	6.3
Fell below the required rate of return on assets	4	3.6	3.6
Would not personally guarantee the finance	4	3.6	3.6
Insufficient information provided by the business	3	2.7	2.7
Poor credit experience or history	2	1.8	1.8
Low personal net worth	2	1.8	1.8
Management team too inexperienced	2	1.8	1.8
Business plan not acceptable	1	0.9	0.9
Other reason	6	5.4	5.4
Total	112	100.0	100.0

Barriers to Development of SMEs

Table 5.5 shows that the overwhelming factor restricting the development of their businesses, in the estimation of SMEs, is the high cost of finance. Other important reasons are the difficulty in accessing credit and the high level of taxation.

These responses confirm that in the perception of SMEs the high cost of credit, the difficulty in accessing credit and the high level of taxation are the three most important barriers to their development. This should signal that if this sector is to expand then priority needs to be given to alleviating these difficulties by removing the barriers, or at least making them less of a hindrance. An acknowledgement that these are 'market conditions' does nothing to alleviate the problems. A notable discouragement is the low level of support to SMEs from local authorities. This highlights the need for greater awareness of the need for local governments to play a more active role in assisting SMEs to start, develop and expand their businesses. The lack of managerial skills is the eighth ranked hindrance to the development of SMEs

Table 5.5: Barriers to the Development of SMEs

N = 124

	Responses		Percentage of cases
	N	Percentage	
Barriers to the development of SMEs			
Cost of borrowing money too high	102	14.0	82.3
Difficulty in accessing credit	86	11.8	69.4
High level of taxation	72	9.9	58.1
Insufficient level of support from local authorities	69	9.5	55.6
Low purchasing power of the population	50	6.9	40.3
Lack of clear governmental SME programme	48	6.6	38.7
Lack of qualified human resources	46	6.3	37.1
Lack of managerial skills	45	6.2	36.3
Lengthy procedures for starting a company	40	5.5	32.3
Lack of proper marketing skills	39	5.4	31.5
Poor co-ordination among organisations supporting SMEs	38	5.2	30.6
Lack of market information	31	4.3	25.0
Negative image of local authorities	23	3.2	18.5
Uncompetitive product	22	3.0	17.7
Other reason	16	2.2	12.9
Total	727	100.0	

Support Required from Government

The main support required by SMEs of government is to facilitate access to finance (75.4%). The reduction of taxation and the publication of information for small businesses follow as the next most significant measures which would help SMEs. Notable among the responses, and cited by 58 per cent of respondents, is the need for governments to create a one-stop shop for SMEs. This highlights the feeling that there is a lack of direction and co-ordination of assistance to SMEs in their attempts to create and generate business. Table 5.6 sets out responses on this issue in greater detail.

Table 5.6: Governmental Measures Required to Support SMEs

N = 107

	Responses		Percentage of cases
	N	Percentage	
Governmental support required for SMEs			
Facilitate access to finance (creation of an SME fund)	89	19.7	75.4
Reduce taxation	76	16.9	64.4
Publish more information for small businesses	69	15.3	58.5
Help to create a one-stop shop for SMEs	67	14.9	56.8
Decrease the number of taxes and simplify the system	61	13.5	51.7
Simplify the registration of new companies	40	8.9	33.9
Create a programme for supporting business women	25	5.5	21.2
Give priority to enterprises owned by women	9	2.0	7.6
Other	15	3.3	12.7
Total	451	100.0	

Areas in which Assistance Is Required

SMEs were asked to state what kind of assistance they would require in making an application for a loan from a financial institution to finance a new expansion project. The responses of the 107 SMEs which answered this question showed that by far the greatest need is for the preparation of a feasibility study, followed by information on markets and marketing requirements. This need does not change materially with the size of the business measured by its assets as can be seen in Table A5.3 of Appendix 2. Nor does it change materially when related to the educational level of business owners, as shown by Table A5.4 of Appendix 2. The preparation of a feasibility study, together with the preparation of a business plan (the third ranked need), appear to be crucial concerns of SMEs that could be met by concerned institutions mounting training programmes at convenient intervals at an affordable cost.

Sixty-one respondents who sought finance answered the question as to whether they had any difficulty completing the application process. Of these, 80 per cent had no difficulty. Table 5.7 shows the type of difficulties encountered by the remaining 20 per cent.

Table 5.7: Difficulties Encountered in the Application Process

N = 12

	Responses		Percentage of cases
	N	Percentage	
Difficulties encountered in the application process			
Too much information required	10	55.6	83.3
Needed further explanation of terms and conditions	2	11.1	16.7
Could not obtain information required	2	11.1	16.7
Could not provide a business plan or future projections	1	5.6	8.3
Did not have any accounting records	1	5.6	8.3
Other	2	11.1	16.7
Total	18	100.0	

However, when businesses were asked in which of a number of areas they would require assistance in making application for a loan to finance a new expansion project, a significant number expressed difficulties in almost all areas of the process (see Table 5.8).

Table 5.8: Areas in which Assistance Was Required in Making a Loan Application

N = 107

	Responses		Percentage of cases
	N	Percentage	
Areas where assistance was required in making an application			
Preparation of a feasibility study on the business project	64	22.8	59.8
Information on markets and marketing requirements	51	18.1	47.7
Preparation of a business plan	43	15.3	40.2
Preparation and maintenance of financial records	41	14.6	38.3
Information on what is required to fulfil the conditions for the loan	41	14.6	38.3
Preparation of the application for finance	39	13.9	36.4
Other	2	0.7	1.9
Total	281	100.0	

More than one-third said that they would experience difficulty in every aspect of the application process, including the preparation of a formal application. It does not augur well for the rapid growth of SMEs when the fundamental requirements for new project finance are so little known or understood. A need for very specific training is indicated, of which consultancies and business service providers could take advantage. Coupled with the fact that more than 50 per cent of 113 respondents claimed not to know the criteria used by financial institutions in evaluating an application for a long-term loan (see Table A5.5 of Appendix 2), there appears to be a significant gap between the needs of SMEs and the realities of the financial environment in which they operate.

Support Required

When asked if they had ever sought support from any type of business service provider, almost two-thirds of 122 respondents claimed not to have done so (see Table A5.9 of Appendix 2). This suggests that they either do not know such services are available or are unwilling to pay for them. Of those that had used business service providers, the majority (67.5%) had made use of accountants and auditors, and 45 per cent had used law firms. Tables 5.10 and 5.11 show the overall incidence of use of business service providers and the stage at which resort was had to them. Table 5.12 sets out the source of financial advice by gender, showing that within each category women were proportionately more likely to seek support from business service providers, particularly law firms, accountants, and advertising and promotion services, while men were less likely to use them. When they did so, they had resort to law firms and accountants most often.

Table 5.9: Requests for Support

		Frequency	Percentage
Valid	No	81	64.8
	Yes	41	32.8
	Total	122	97.6
Missing	System	3	2.4
Total		125	100.0

Table 5.10: Business Service Providers from Whom Support Was Sought

N = 36

	Responses		Percentage of cases
	N	Percentage	
Organisations from which support was sought			
Accountants and auditors	27	30.7	67.5
Law firms	18	20.5	45.0
Advertising and promotion agencies	14	15.9	35.0
Private consulting firms	10	11.4	25.0
Training service providers	5	5.7	12.5
SME service centres	5	5.7	12.5
Talent market/employment agencies	4	4.5	10.0
Other	5	5.7	12.5
Total	88	100.0	

Table 5.11: Stage at which Businesses Asked for Support

N = 36

		Frequency	Percentage
Valid	During the process of setting up the company	14	11.2
	When the company started to grow	14	11.2
	Before creating the company	8	6.4
	Other	2	1.6
	When the company started having problems	1	0.8
	Total	39	31.2
Missing	System	86	68.8
Total		125	100.0

Most Appropriate Form of Finance

When asked what kind of finance was the most appropriate for their businesses, the need most frequently identified by the respondents (27.4%), was for long-term finance. This was followed by overdraft facilities and lines of credit. Long-term finance in this context should be taken to mean finance for terms of ten years or less as from Figure 5.3 no real preference was expressed for loans of more than ten years. Table 5.13 sets out the priorities expressed in relation to this issue.

Table A5.6 of Appendix 2 shows the preferences of businesses for each type of loan by size, broken down by numbers of employees. Except for businesses of more than 100 employees, more than 62 per cent of businesses of all sizes prefer long-term loans. The largest businesses expressed a preference for demand loans and lines of credit. This is possibly because these are more established businesses and do not need long-term loans for the purchase of equipment or of land and buildings

Table 5.12: Business Service Providers from Whom Support Was Sought by Gender of Owner

N = 36

		Service providers from whom support was sought							
		Law firm	**Private consulting firm**	**Training service provider**	**Talent market/ employment agency**	**SME service centre**	**Accountants and auditors**	**Advertising and promotion service provider**	**Total**
Gender of majority owner									
Male	Number	10	8	2	3	3	17	7	24
	Percentage of group	41.7	33.3	8.3	12.5	12.5	70.8	29.2	
Female	Number	6	2	1	0	2	6	5	8
	Percentage of group	75.0	25.0	12.5	0.0	25.0	75.0	62.5	
Joint	Number	2	0	2	1	0	4	2	4
	Percentage of group	50.0	0	50.0	25.0	0.0	100.0	50.0	
Total	Number	18	10	5	4	5	27	14	36

Table 5.13: Most Appropriate Finance for the Business

N = 122

	Responses		Percentage of cases
	N	Percentage	
Most appropriate finance for business			
Long-term loan	77	27.4	63.1
Overdraft facilities	66	23.5	54.1
Line of credit	46	16.4	37.7
Demand or short-term loan	38	13.5	31.1
Credit card limit	23	8.2	18.9
Equity finance	15	5.3	12.3
Lease of equipment or machinery	14	5.0	11.5
Other	2	0.7	1.6
Total	281	100.0	

When asked what documents could be made immediately available to a financial institution as a requirement for a long-term loan, 24 per cent identified 'a business plan for the next three years', 'the deeds of the business assets' and 'the audited financial statements for the last two years'. Table 5.14 shows the dispersion of responses to this question.

Table 5.14: Documents Immediately Available to Support an Application for a Long-term Loan

N = 123

	Responses		Percentage of cases
	N	Percentage	
Document availability for a long-term loan			
A business plan for the next three years	78	24.0	63.4
Title deeds of the business assets as collateral for a loan	78	24.0	63.4
Audited financial statements for the last two years	77	23.7	62.6
Title deeds of the assets of the owner of the business as collateral for a loan	56	17.2	45.5
A feasibility study for a business proposal	36	11.1	29.3
Total	325	100.0	

In view of the need respondents expressed for assistance in preparing a business plan when making an application for a loan, these responses must be taken to mean that these documents could be made available on request and not necessarily that they are available.

More than two-thirds of the respondents who answered the question as to whether they knew how to attract equity finance from an investor said that they did not know (Table 5.15).

Table 5.15: Knowledge of How Businesses Can Attract Equity Finance

		Frequency	Percentage	Valid percentage	Cumulative percentage
Valid	No	81	64.8	68.1	68.1
	Yes	38	30.4	31.9	100.0
	Total	119	95.2	100.0	
Missing	System	6	4.8		
Total		125	100.0		

Table 5.16: Knowledge of Conditions and Standards Needed for Competition in International Markets

		Health (in food processing)	Packaging	Presentation	Product specification	Quality
N	Valid	15	77	95	96	106
	Yes	11	39	61	54	69
	Percentage of Total	73.3	50.6	64.2	56.3	65.1
	No	4	38	34	42	37
	Percentage of Total	26.7	49.4	35.8	43.7	34.9
	Missing	110	48	30	29	19

There seem to be considerable deficiencies in knowledge of international conditions and standards on almost all parameters tested, as can be seen from Table 5.16. Between 25 and 50 per cent of respondents did not know of these standards. This is particularly so in terms of packaging.

Main Problems Encountered by Businesses

Table 5.17 shows that SMEs regard the lack of long-term finance as the major problem facing them. Closely following on this is a shortage of skilled workers. There is also a need for other forms of finance and for readily available and affordable consulting services. SMEs also feel that there is a scarcity of affordable managerial skills, lack of access to foreign markets and no association which represents their interests. Other areas complained of where opportunities exist for improving the rate of development of SMEs were:

- Access to appropriate technology
- Unfavourable tax barriers

- Access to public contracts
- An unfavourable legal system

These warrant further investigation, as many of them represent areas where governments could improve the conditions under which SMEs operate.

Table 5.17: Main Problems Encountered by Businesses

N = 118

	Responses		Percentage of cases
	N	Percentage	
Main problems encountered by businesses			
Lack of long-term finance	63	11.6	53.4
Inadequate skilled labour force	62	11.5	52.5
Lack of other forms of finance	37	6.8	31.4
Lack of readily available and affordable consulting services	35	6.5	29.7
Scarcity of affordable management skills	34	6.3	28.8
Access to foreign markets	33	6.1	28.0
Absence of an association to represent SMEs' business interests	33	6.1	28.0
Lack of access to appropriate technology required to support the business	31	5.7	26.3
Unfavourable tax barriers or tariffs	27	5.0	22.9
Lack of access to public contracts and sub-contracts	26	4.8	22.0
Unfavourable legal system (costly, slow and unpredictable)	26	4.8	22.0
No access to international partners	25	4.6	21.2
Inadequacy of production inputs in terms of quality	24	4.4	20.3
Inadequate transportation services	20	3.7	16.9
Foreign exchange restrictions	18	3.3	15.3
Inadequate channels of distribution	17	3.1	14.4
Regulatory or legal requirements or constraints	15	2.8	12.7
Unable to meet standards of international markets	8	1.5	6.8
Other	7	1.3	5.9
Total	541	100.0	

6

Skills and Training Needs of SMEs

Training Programmes Attended

Table 6.1 shows the low level of attendance at training programmes of the most fundamental nature. All areas, except that of strategic planning, disclose a paucity of training among the managements of SMEs. Together with the low level of responses from the businesses surveyed, training does not appear to be a high priority among SMEs, or it is unavailable at an affordable cost.

Table 6.1: Training Programmes Attended

N = 88

	Responses		Percentage of cases
	N	Percentage	
Training programmes attended			
Strategic planning	62	23.0	70.5
The taxation of businesses	43	15.9	48.9
Interviewing and evaluation techniques	35	13.0	39.8
Project evaluation and review	32	11.9	36.4
Company secretarial practice	28	10.4	31.8
Preparing minutes and reports	24	8.9	27.3
Incorporating a company	23	8.5	26.1
The use and application of codes of conduct in business	23	8.5	26.1
Total	270	100.0	

Training Programmes Required

Table 6.2 shows the types of training programmes in which SMEs have indicated an interest. Prominent among them is modern management principles and practices, followed by sources of finance. Management skills and knowledge of the sources of finance therefore appear to be the principal knowledge deficiencies among SMEs.

Table 6.2: Training Programmes Businesses Would Make Use of If They Were Available

N = 122

	Responses		Percentage of cases
	N	Percentage	
Training programmes to which businesses would subscribe			
Modern management principles and practices	74	8.4	60.7
Sources of finance	69	7.8	56.6
Best practices in sales and marketing	68	7.7	55.7
Strategic planning	61	6.9	50.0
Entrepreneurship	52	5.9	42.6
Use of the Internet in the promotion of businesses	47	5.3	38.5
Methods of compiling business plans	46	5.2	37.7
The preparation of feasibility studies	46	5.2	37.7
Credit providers and their requirements	45	5.1	36.9
Best practices in recruitment, employment and labour relations	44	5.0	36.1
Interviewing and evaluation techniques	43	4.9	35.2
Information technology use in start-up enterprises	42	4.8	34.4
Business taxation	42	4.8	34.4
Production of goods and services	34	3.9	27.9
Accounting knowledge and systems appropriate for start-up operations	33	3.7	27.0
The nature of a venture enterprise	31	3.5	25.4
The use, design, and presentation of exhibitions	31	3.5	25.4
Project evaluation and review	23	2.6	18.9
Public offerings of stock	15	1.7	12.3
Incorporating a company	15	1.7	12.3
Preparing minutes and reports	12	1.4	9.8
Recycling practices	8	0.9	6.6
Total	881	100.0	

IV Lenders' Experience of the Financing of SMEs

A survey of lenders' experiences of making long-term loans to SMEs was conducted simultaneously with the SME survey. Thirty-two responses from eight CARICOM countries were received. The results are tabulated below and in Appendix 3. Efforts were made to access a range of lending institutions in as many of the countries in which the SME survey was conducted as possible. In the event, no lending institution approached in Antigua and Barbados would participate in the survey.

7

Business Characteristics of Lenders

Figure 7.1 shows the distribution of responses by country and Figure 7.2 shows the types of lending institutions that responded. Of the 'other financial institutions' that responded, five were micro-finance organisations, one was a building society, one was a non-governmental organisation and one was a mutual fund.

Figure 7.1: Distribution of Lending Institutions by Country

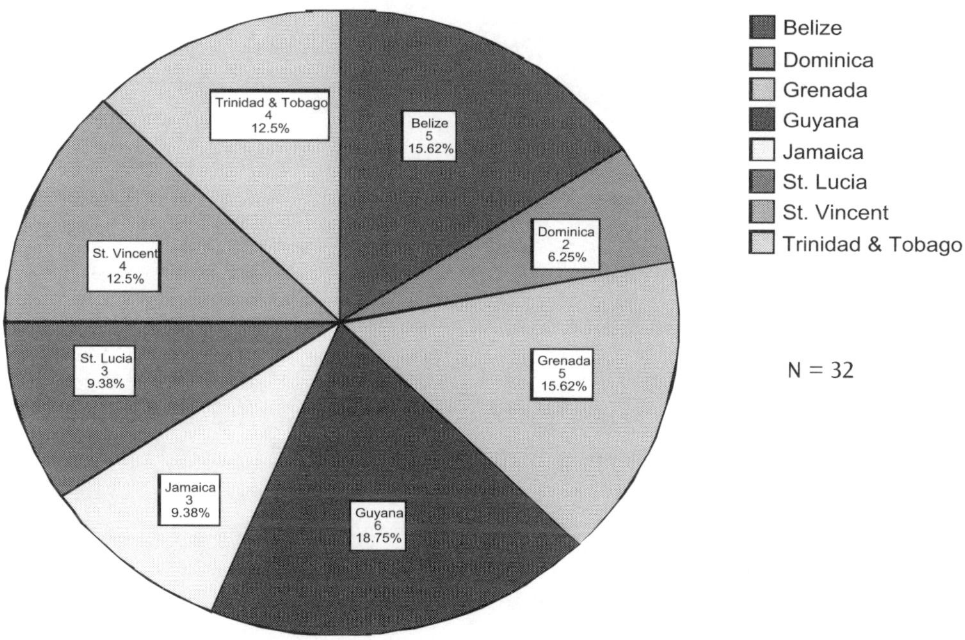

Of the companies surveyed, 59 per cent made long-term finance available to SMEs, and 41 per cent did not. The latter, however, provided SMEs with other forms of finance. Table A1.1 of Appendix 3 shows the types of finance made available by financial institutions to SMEs. In 97 per cent of cases, short-term loans were available, followed by mortgage loans, new lines of credit and increases in credit card limits. Long-term loans other than mortgage loans were available in 48 per cent of cases. In terms of requests, however, most were for short-term loans, but long-term loans were, as shown in Table A1.2 of Appendix 3, the next most often requested, followed by mortgage loans.

Figure 7.2: Types of Lending Institutions

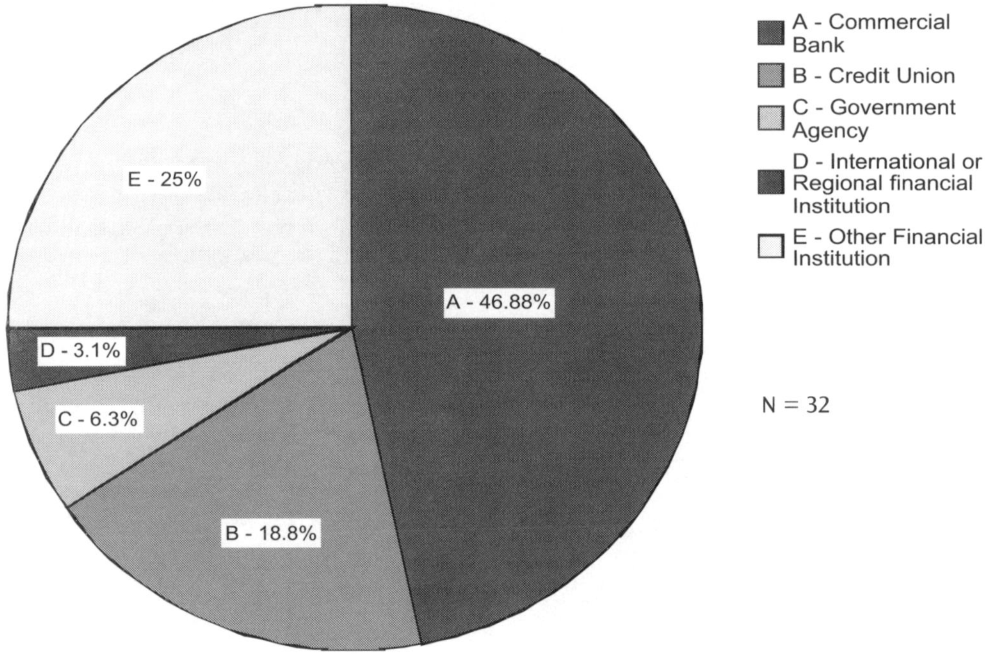

Table A1.3 of Appendix 3 shows the distribution of financial institutions providing long-term finance. The results show that 19 (59%) of the 32 financial institutions that responded provided long-term finance. Of these, 10 (52.6%) were banks. Three (15.8%) were credit unions. The others were a government agency, an international agency and four micro-finance organisations.

Table A1.4 of Appendix 3 shows that the sectors in which businesses requesting finance operated were, in order of importance, agriculture, fisheries, tourism and food processing.

Tables A1.5 and A1.6 of Appendix 3 show the mean and modal, minimum and maximum amounts of finance requested by SMEs by sector from all financial institutions. Table 1.7 of Appendix 3 shows that the highest mean loan term requested by sector was ten years. In only two cases did the maximum terms of loans requested exceed this mean. These were in the tourism and food processing sectors.

Evaluation of Requests for Finance

Lenders were asked to indicate what documents were required in the application process. Sixty-three per cent of the companies surveyed responded to this inquiry. Of these, the great majority required the business and personal financial statements of the SMEs, followed by appraisals of assets provided as collateral, a business plan and cash flow projections. As we have already noted, these requirements are among those with which more than one-third of SMEs wanted assistance in making an application to finance a new project.

Table 7.1: Documents Requested in the Application Process

N = 20

	Responses		Percentage of cases
	N	Percentage	
Documents requested in the application process			
Business financial statement	19	13.0	95.0
Appraisals of assets to be financed	18	12.3	90.0
Business plan	18	12.3	90.0
Cash flow projection	18	12.3	90.0
Formal application for finance	18	12.3	90.0
Personal financial statement	18	12.3	90.0
Audited financial statement of the business	17	11.6	85.0
Franchise agreement	9	6.2	45.0
No documentation is requested.	2	1.4	10.0
Other documentation	9	6.2	45.0
Total	146	100.0	

Table 7.2 shows that lenders who actually provide long-term finance regard the credit risk of the entity as the highest priority among the many factors that they take into account when advancing long-term loans to SMEs. The soundness of the business plan and the extent of the owner's contribution to the enterprise are the next major considerations, followed closely by the reliability of the borrowing entity. Economic and political considerations do not appear to play a very significant role in the evaluation of loan applications.

Table 7.3 shows other significant considerations that financial institutions take into account when evaluating an application for finance. As will be seen, the competitiveness of the enterprise and its marketing advantage play significant roles. The availability of applicable technology and labour skills are also important considerations.

Table 7.2: Factors Taken into Account by Lenders in Advancing Long-term Loans

N = 32

Priorities	Valid	1st	2nd	3rd	4th	5th	6th	7th	8th	9th	10th	11th
1. Economic environment	17	1	0	1	4	2	6	1		2	0	0
2. Political environment	14	0	0	0	1		1		3	1	5	2
3. Credit risk	18	11	4	2	1	0	0	0	0	0	0	0
4. Interest rate risk	17	1	2	2	1	5	1	3	2	0	0	0
5. Purchasing power risk	14	1	1	1	2	2	5	2	0	0	0	0
6. Reliability of the borrowing entity	19	3	4	2	3	2	2	3	0	0	0	0
7. Motivation of the management of the borrowing entity	17	2	2	5	0	0	4	3	0	0	1	0
8. Soundness of the business plan presented	19	2	7	3	3	2		2	0	0	0	0
9. Extent of owner's contribution to the enterprise	19	0	3	8	2	2	1	1	1	0	0	0
10. Local knowledge and connections of the investor	17	0	0	0	2	1	0	6				
11. The applicant is a customer of the institution	14	2	0	0	0	1	0	2	0	3	2	3
Other	1											

Table 7.3: Other Considerations in Evaluating an Application for Finance

N = 19

	Responses		Percentage of cases
	N	Percentage	
Matters considered in evaluating applications			
Competitiveness of the enterprise	18	11.0	94.7
Niche market for product	17	10.4	89.5
Availability of applicable technology	17	10.4	89.5
Labour force skill	17	10.4	89.5
Deficiencies in investor knowledge	14	8.5	73.7
Labour force reliability	14	8.5	73.7
Compliance with export /import non-tariff regulations	12	7.3	63.2
Reliability of transportation (land and sea)	12	7.3	63.2
Reliability of utilities	12	7.3	63.2
Reliability of telecommunication technology	11	6.7	57.9
Labour cost stability	11	6.7	57.9
Taxation	9	5.5	47.4
Total	164	100.0	

Other Business Characteristics

Table 7.4 shows the factors that lenders regard as important when considering an application for finance. The most important, so far as the business's performance is concerned, are the rate of growth in sales and whether the business has expanded in the last five years through the re-investment of its income. It is clear that the essential fundamentals of the business weigh heavily with lenders when they are considering applications for finance. An interesting factor which is of importance to lenders is whether the enterprise has prior outstanding loans from other lenders. This is possibly because the existence of prior loans is considered to be an indication of the enterprise's ability to repay its debts. The qualifications of the senior managers of the enterprise are also of great concern to lenders, who no doubt wish to be assured that the management of the enterprise is in knowledgeable and experienced hands.

Table 7.4: Important Factors in the Decision to Provide Long-term Finance

N = 20

	Very important	Important	Fairly important	Quite important	Unimportant
Factors of importance to decision to provide long-term finance					
The product of the enterprise is for export	4	3	3	3	7
The enterprise has shown strong sales growth in the last two years	11	6	2	1	0
The lender's relationship with the enterprise has extended for more than five years	6	6	5	2	0
The enterprise has prior outstanding loans from other parties	8	6	1	3	1
The enterprise has a high degree of liquidity	5	9	4	2	0
The enterprise has a low debt-to-assets ratio	7	7	5	1	
The qualifications of the senior managers of the enterprise in matters of finance appear to be weak	8	6	4	1	1
The enterprise has expanded its business over the last five years through the re-investment of its net income	10	8	1	0	1

Security Required

Table 7.5: Form of Security Required by Lenders when Examining an Application for Long-term Finance

N = 19

Guarantee required	Frequency	Percentage
Bank guarantee	3	9.4
Owners' guarantee	16	50.0
Mortgage of SME's fixed assets	19	59.4
Hypothecation of securities	14	43.8
Government guarantee	0	0.0
Guarantee of an international or regional organisation	0	0.0
Other form of security	5	15.6

Mortgages of fixed assets and securities and owners' guarantees are the most frequently required items of security requested by financial institutions. Table 7.6 reveals that lenders most often require the owners of businesses to pledge as security their business assets, although a large number also required the personal assets of the owners to be offered as security for finance. SMEs, on the other hand, reported that the personal assets of the business owners were most often required as security for long-term loans.

Table 7.6: Collateral for Long-term Finance Required by Lenders

	Frequency	Percentage of sample	Valid percentage
Business Assets N = 18			
Yes	15	46.9	83.3
No	3	9.4	16.7
Total	18	56.3	100.0
Personal Assets N = 16			
Yes	11	34.4	68.8
No	5	15.6	31.3
Total	16	50.0	100.0

Reasons for Refusing Finance

Table 7.7: Typical Reasons for Refusing Financing

	Responses		Percentage of cases
	N	Percentage	
Typical reasons for turning down loan applications			
Insufficient income or revenue or sales to service financing	17	11.5	94.4
Insufficient cash flow	16	10.8	88.9
Poor credit experience or history	16	10.8	88.9
Insufficient information provided by the business	15	10.1	83.3
Business plan not acceptable	14	9.5	77.8
Insufficient collateral/security	14	9.5	77.8
The management team was too inexperienced	13	8.8	72.2
Insufficient equity	13	8.8	72.2
Insufficient working capital	9	6.1	50.0
Fell below the required rate of return on assets	9	6.1	50.0
Low personal net worth	7	4.7	38.9
Would not personally guarantee the finance	5	3.4	27.8
Total	148	100.0	

When asked what, in their opinion, were the typical reasons why applications for long-term loans were declined, the majority of financial institutions thought it was because there was 'insufficient income to service the loan', followed by 'insufficient cash flow', 'poor credit experience' and 'insufficient information provided by the enterprise'. This accords well with the answers provided by SMEs as to the reasons why their requests for finance were declined, as shown in Table 2.8. Table 7.7 shows that 'insufficient cash flow' and 'the inadequacy of information provided by the business' were highly ranked factors cited by both SMEs and lenders. However, while the insufficiency of collateral was the second most highly ranked reason by SMEs, it tied for fifth place among the reasons given by lenders.

Very few of the financial institutions provided information about the average percentage of applications approved and declined. Of the few that did, Table A2.1 of Appendix 3 sets out the mean and modal percentages of applications declined by sector in the estimation of financial institutions. The most frequently encountered mode is 20 per cent for most sectors. This appears to be a rather generous under-estimate compared to the actual experience of SMEs. Table A2.2 of Appendix 3 shows that nearly 43 per cent of financial institutions estimated the failure rate of business loans at 5–9 per cent and another 25 per cent of financial institutions estimated that the failure rate was under 5 per cent. If correct, these are reasonably acceptable numbers for the delinquency rate of loans to businesses of this size.

Opportunities for Reducing Risk

A number of questions were posed to financial institutions on the subject of reducing their risk exposure if finance was made available to them by the international finance institutions (IFIs) for on-lending. The responses are set out in Table 7.8. These show that financial institutions are prepared to assist SMEs in their approaches for finance and are more prepared to share the risk through debt finance than through equity participation.

Table 7.8: Risk Reduction Alternatives

	N		Yes	Percentage
	Valid	Missing		
Actively seek out such enterprises for funding	28	4	25	78.1
Assess business cases as presented and recommend assistance in the preparation of a business plan	27	5	25	78.1
Provide normal banking services and facilities to the entity on a 'most-favoured customer' basis	24	8	19	59.4
Share the risk with an IFI which would provide a guarantee for a portion of the loan	22	10	18	56.3
Share the risk with an IFI which would undertake a portion of the debt finance	24	8	22	68.8
Share the risk with an IFI which would invest in a portion of the equity of the enterprise	22	10	12	37.5
Provide full accounting and regular reporting to the International Agency	25	7	23	71.9

When asked to indicate their preference for various risk-sharing approaches in local or foreign currencies and at domestic or international market-related rates depending on who takes the foreign exchange risk, a clear preference was expressed for funds to be made available to SMEs in domestic currency at domestic market rates, with the IFI taking the foreign exchange risk. These preferences are expressed in Table 7.9. As international market-related rates are lower than domestic rates, some explanation of this preference is needed.

Table 7.9 Funding Preferences for SMEs

Funding preferences for SMEs	N		Yes	Percentage
	Valid	Missing		
An IFI to make funds available and repayable in foreign currency at international market-related rates (with the enterprise taking the foreign exchange risk)	2	30	2	6.3
An IFI to make funds available and repayable in foreign currency at domestic market-related interest rates (the enterprise taking the foreign exchange risk)	1	31	1	3.1
An IFI to make funds available and repayable in domestic currency at domestic market-r elated interest rates (with the IFI taking the foreign exchange risks)	14	18	14	43.8
An IFI to make funds available and repayable in domestic currency at international market-related interest rates (with the IFI taking the foreign exchange risk)	6	26	5	15.6
A mixture of the above, wholly or partially in foreign currency /domestic currency	7	25	7	21.9

Conclusion

The objective of the study was to determine what, if any, impediments existed to access to long-term finance by SMEs, what these impediments were and how they could be overcome. A secondary, but related, objective was to ascertain what, in the perceptions of SMEs, were the obstacles to their development. It is evident from the findings of the study that many SMEs have not accessed long-term finance either because they do not need it or because, for various reasons, they think that it is unavailable. Of the SMEs that needed long-term finance, 30 per cent were unable to obtain it. The major obstacles to access are the requirement for collateral, insufficient equity, insufficient cash flow and the high cost of debt finance. More significant, however, is the finding that nearly half the financial institutions surveyed did not provide long-term finance to SMEs. This could be a major and serious obstacle to these enterprises gaining access to such finance. From the lenders' perspective, the low level of access was related to SMEs' low level of cash flow and insufficient collateral. No doubt these are standard market considerations when assessing loan requests. More to the point, however, is the fact that only 41 per cent of all businesses surveyed availed themselves of opportunities for accessing some form of finance. The need for long-term finance, therefore, appears to be a significant concern for SMEs.

As regards impediments to the development of SMEs, the first observation must be the low level of entrepreneurship in the communities concerned. The small number of businesses whose owners are aged between 18 and 30, or who are women, provides back-up for this observation. Most (74%) SMEs have been in business for over five years, while over 50 per cent have been in business for more than ten years. Eighty-nine per cent of business owners are over 30 years of age and 71 per cent are over 40 years of age. So there is scope for encouraging young people to go into business and for increasing the level of female ownership of businesses. The educational level of business owners does not appear to be an impediment to doing business, nor does the self-assessed competence of owners in various managerial functions. The confidence of owners in their expertise must emanate from their experience of doing business as very few have had the benefit of specific management training. Moreover, more than 50 per cent have indicated the need for training in modern management practices, sources of finance and best practices in sales and marketing. Whether entrepreneurship can be taught is a question that has always been open to debate, but there have been some attempts in this regard, particularly in Japan.

These findings provide a base for the following observations:

1. There is need for governments to provide, as a matter of course, training programmes and workshops free of charge or at minimal cost to SMEs in the following areas: business essentials; business planning; marketing your business; business finance; business

procurement; doing business with the government; and entrepreneurship.

2. There is a need for governments to provide bureaus where SMEs can access specific assistance in such matters as the preparation of business plans, production of feasibility studies and completion of loan application forms. Opportunities should also be arranged for SMEs to meet lenders in forums, so that the requirements and expectations of the latter can be better communicated, as well as the needs of the SMEs.

3. Arrangements could be made to provide both long- and short-term financial support on affordable terms to SMEs that demonstrate a competence in utilising such finance either by their past track record or by attending pre-determined training programmes relevant to their businesses and needs. This could be seen as an attempt to get around the requirement for collateral while also minimising the credit risk.

4. A way should be found to provide incentives, through recognition and tax relief, to lenders who demonstrate a consistent support for SMEs by making access to finance more readily available or otherwise providing the support necessary to facilitate this.

5. IFIs can play an effective role in promoting SMEs by contributing to reducing the risk exposure of local financial institutions and by funding appropriate business services through technical assistance.

Appendix 1

Survey Methodology and Experience of Researchers

It was decided to conduct the survey in the largest CARICOM counties, i.e. Guyana, Belize, Jamaica, Trinidad and Tobago, and Barbados, and two countries each in the Windward and Leeward Islands – St Lucia, Grenada, Antigua and Dominica. An additional country, St Vincent, was also included in case the responses from the Windward Islands proved unsatisfactory. The choice of countries was made on the basis of the known extent of economic activity in the region; it also sought to capture a representative sample of all the countries in CARICOM geographically.

The businesses selected for the survey were intended to fall within the category of 'small and medium-sized' businesses. 'Small and medium-sized' must be read conjunctively and not disjunctively, as despite efforts to identify businesses by size, there was no database from which to do so. In the absence of a database, no random sample could be taken and researchers in each country had to identify businesses based on their personal knowledge of the sizes of businesses and by using information gleaned from the records of employer organisations and the knowledge of informed persons operating in the field. It was finally decided to target businesses using the following criteria:

1. Businesses that employed between five and 100 people;
2. Businesses that had assets or revenue of between US$100,000 and US$1 million;
3. Businesses that were spread over 14 economic sectors.

Researchers attempted to select businesses by size equitably within predetermined ranges, varying both by number of employees and by assets. This proved impractical in most countries as the overwhelming number of businesses had less than 25 employees. The attempt to sample a representative number of businesses by size was therefore superseded by a selection more nearly based on the actual dispersion of businesses by size in each country.

The sectors were identified in accordance with the types of businesses most frequently catered for by the Caribbean Development Bank in its Caribbean Technological Consultancy Services programme for SMEs. Here again, because of the lack of adequate pre-existing data, it was not possible to sample an equal number from each sector, although the researchers tried to ensure that all sectors were represented. As was to be expected, the sectors which were most frequently sampled were those that were the most dominant in the economies of the countries concerned.

The types of financial institutions operating in the field of providing finance to businesses were noted on a visit to three of the countries selected for the survey, Barbados, Trinidad and Tobago, and Guyana. Discussions were held with one regional financial institution, two private sector financial institutions, three employers' organisations, one regional employers' association and three SMEs. Discussions at a meeting of regional agencies arranged by the Caribbean Development Bank and the Caribbean Export Development Agency also proved useful in providing background information for the study. From these discussions it was possible to identify the institutions providing finance in the region and obtain references to them. The opportunity was also taken to impress on the employers' associations the usefulness of the survey and to engage their support, and through them the support of their membership, for the completion of the questionnaires.

There appeared to be no prior studies of this nature in the Caribbean to which reference could be made for purposes of comparison, and therefore the study appears to have broken new ground.

The questionnaires were designed after reference to similar recent studies in Canada and the UK. Many adaptations had to be made because of the differences in the terms of reference and objectives of those studies. However, they proved to be helpful in focusing the questions on the essential areas of inquiry. While it was recognised that surveys of this nature imposed quite heavily on the time and resources of the businesses surveyed, opportunity was taken to inquire into several areas beyond the narrow confines of the terms of reference in order to capture the wider context in which SMEs operate and to obtain their views on how the economic environment affects their development efforts.

The SME questionnaire was sent to five enterprises initially to determine if it was logical in its presentation and whether the recipients had any difficulties in completing it. Three of the five responded by completing the questionnaire and returning it with their comments. After some amendments, the final version of the questionnaire was submitted to the Commonwealth Secretariat for further review, and agreed.

Researchers in the field were required to identify the businesses to be surveyed and make initial contact with them through introductory letters furnished by the Commonwealth Secretariat and the consultant, explaining the origins of the survey and its objectives and soliciting their support. These introductory letters were followed up with visits by researchers to the enterprises where they explained the nature of the questionnaire and left it to be completed within a specified time. Follow-up calls were then made to each business to ask whether they needed assistance in the completion of the questionnaire. Where such assistance was requested, the researcher returned to inquire into the nature of the difficulties encountered and tried to resolve them. Questionnaires were then collected by the researchers and reviewed for completeness.

The completion of the questionnaires was conducted over a six-week period from 1 October to 12 November 2005. One hundred and fifty questionnaires were returned by SMEs, of which 125 were useable. Thirty-eight questionnaires from lenders were returned, of which 32 were useable.

The experience of the researchers was varied and in many cases taxing. A number of businesses declined to participate for various reasons, most of which reflected their lack of confidence that the findings would be put to any useful purpose. Some felt that the disclosure of their financial circumstances could be a security risk. Not all businesses that declined to participate were as polite as might have been wished in expressing their lack of interest in the survey or reasons for not participating.

Below is a sample of some of the comments of the researchers reflecting their experience in arranging for the completion of the questionnaires.

Question:
What were the most frequently encountered reasons for declining to complete the questionnaire?

Answers:
1. The questions were asking for private financial information about the individual and the company. Respondents were not comfortable with sharing this information, despite the fact that some of these questions were optional, they were being completed anonymously and that responses would be reported in the aggregate.

2. 'Survey fatigue' and 'lack of time' were the most common reasons given. Business owners were tired of completing surveys and not seeing any results. This was most acute in terms of the manufacturers.

Question:
What were the main difficulties experienced by the researcher in carrying out the assignment?

Answers:
1. Bureaucracy within the large organisations, that is, the suppliers of credit.

2. Finding businesses to match the criteria and accessing the owners. Owners were reluctant to share financial, information, especially when they had to identify themselves. Some refused to take part because they had no guarantee that they would not be identified them at a later point. The time of the year meant that only a short time was given, as owners were busy planning for the Christmas shopping season.

And from a financial institution, when requested to participate in the survey:

> 'I think the market is served in a satisfactory manner. Sometimes SMEs need some assistance in preparing business and marketing plans. Not all banks have the same lending policies but I believe that if a proposal makes good business sense it will eventually get financing.
> 'At the moment I have an audit from the Central Bank, and I am also preparing budgets and strategic plans. Your questionnaire is quite detailed and I certainly do not have the time to reply to you at this time. I wish you good luck in your research.'

These replies were repeated in almost all territories and represent the most frequently encountered responses to the researchers' attempts to arrange for the questionnaires to be completed. In addition, some businesses returned the questionnaires with uncomplimentary remarks about its ultimate use.

The same procedures were used with regard to the lenders' questionnaires. Some researchers were unable to secure a full complement of 20 responses from SMEs from each country and six from suppliers of credit. Nor were they able to encourage lenders in all the countries where SMEs were surveyed to participate. Nevertheless, given the circumstances and the time limit for obtaining responses to questionnaires, the researchers did a commendable job.

The results were tabulated using the Statistical Programme for the Social Sciences (SPSS 14.0) and the results are reported in the study. A number of tests were identified for reporting and cross tabulations performed to determine the significance of these tests. These are also reported in the study and, where appropriate, comments are made as to their salience and relevance to the objectives of the survey.

In none of the countries surveyed were there any impediments to the movement of money, so that it was possible for both local currency and foreign currency loans to be made. This was not, therefore, seen as an impediment to access to finance by SMEs. All countries had institutional arrangements for businesses to be registered or incorporated, and indeed the majority were incorporated as private companies. Despite these arrangements there were, with few exceptions, no records available of the nature of the enterprises in terms of their size or asset base, even among employers' associations. Where employers' associations had such records, they were mostly to determine contribution rates and not for analytical purposes, and so they were not available.

The report is subject to the usual survey and sampling methodological deficiencies. These occur for many reasons, for example a lack of basic information on which to base the survey, failure to respond, differences in the interpretation of questions and incorrect information from respondents. Time constraints also played an important role in determining how the survey was initiated and conducted.

An initial report was submitted to the Commonwealth Secretariat in November 2005, based on 90 responses to 20 questions asked in the questionnaire. This formed the basis of a report presented to a meeting of financiers held in Barbados in November 2005. Unsurprisingly, the final report does not vary much from the preliminary report on the matters dealt with there, even though it is based on information supplied by 125 respondents.

Appendix 2

Small and Medium-sized Enterprises

Table A1.1: Business Characteristics

All businesses N = 125	**Number in sample**	**Percentage of sample**
Number of Employees		
1–5	32	25.6
6–25	69	55.2
26–50	12	9.6
51–75	4	3.2
76–100	4	3.2
Over 100	3	2.4
Turnover		
Under US$100,000	36	28.8
US$100,001–US$200,000	31	24.8
US$200,001–US$500,000	15	12.0
US$500,001–US$1 million	14	11.2
Over US$1 million	21	16.8
Assets		
Under US$100,000	34	27.2
US$100,001–US$200,000	25	20.0
US$200,001–US$500,000	25	20.0
US$500,001–US$1 million	15	12.0
Over US$1 million	24	19.2
Sector		
Accounting, computerisation and financial services	7	5.6
Agro industry, fisheries and livestock	8	6.4
Building material, construction, machinery and manufacturing	10	8.0
Distributors	17	13.6
Food processing	16	12.8
Hospitality	14	11.2
Pottery, ceramics, glass, jewellery and craft manufacturing	2	1.6
Printing publishing, packaging and labelling	6	4.8
Services	37	29.6
Shipping, storage and warehousing	3	2.4
Textiles	1	0.8
Wood and metal fabrication	4	3.2

Table A1.1: Business Characteristics (continued)

All businesses N = 125	**Number in sample**	**Percentage of sample**
Country		
Antigua	4	3.2
Barbados	11	8.8
Belize	21	16.8
Dominica	9	7.2
Grenada	21	16.8
Guyana	12	9.6
Jamaica	8	6.4
St Lucia	11	8.8
St Vincent	9	7.2
Trinidad and Tobago	19	15.2
Legal form		
Private corporation	76	60.8
Public corporation	3	2.4
Sole proprietorship	35	28.0
Partnership	10	8.0
Gender ownership		
Male	89	71.2
Female	19	15.2
Joint	15	12.0
Origin of business		
Started from scratch	110	88.0
Took over family business	9	7.2
Purchased an existing business	5	4.0
Spin-off from another business	1	0.8
Sales growth last year		
Sales grew moderately	58	46.4
Sales grew slowly	37	29.65
Sales grew rapidly	13	10.4
Sales decreased	8	6.4
Sales did not grow	5	4.0
Expected future sales growth		
Somewhat stronger	53	42.4
About the same	30	24.0
Much stronger	24	19.2
Somewhat weaker	10	8.0
Much weaker	5	4.0
Original base at home		
Yes	64	51.2
No	47	37.6

Table A1.1: Business Characteristics (continued)

All businesses N = 125	**Number in sample**	**Percentage of sample**
Years in business		
<3 years	18	14.7
3–5 years	14	11.5
6–9 years	27	22.1
10–19 years	34	27.8
Over 20 years	29	23.7

Table A1.2: Characteristics of Principal Owners

Category	**Number in sample**	**Percentage of sample**
Gender		
Male	89	71.2
Female	19	15.2
Joint	15	12.0
Age		
1–29	2	1.6
30–39	22	17.6
40–64	89	71.2
Over 65	12	9.6
Highest academic qualification		
Primary school	3	2.4
Secondary school	23	18.4
Technical/vocational	29	23.2
University degree	50	40.0
Post-graduate degree	18	14.4
Experience		
Less than 5 years	10	8.0
6–8 years	13	10.4
9–15 years	22	17.6
16–20 years	28	22.4
Over 20 years	52	41.6

Table A1.3: Distribution of Businesses (Number of Employees) by Product Type

Number of employees Sector	1–5	6–25	26–50	51–75	76–100	More than 100	Total
Accounting, computerisation and financial services	2	5	0	0	0	0	7
Services	8	23	2	2	2	0	37
Shipping, storage and warehousing	1	2	0	0	0	0	3
Textiles	0	1	0	0	0	0	1
Wood and metal fabrication	0	2	0	0	0	2	4
Agro industry, fisheries and livestock	4	2	0	1	0	0	7
Building material, construction, machinery and manufacturing	1	7	0	0	1	1	10
Distributors	5	8	4	0	0	0	17
Food processing	7	5	3	1	0	0	16
Hospitality	3	8	2	0	1	0	14
Pottery, ceramics, glass, jewellery and craft manufacturing	0	2	0	0	0	0	2
Printing and publishing,	1	4	1	0	0	0	6
Total	32	69	12	4	4	3	124

Table A1.4: Distribution of Businesses (Number of Employees) by Years in Business

		Years in Business					Total
		<3	3–5	6–9	10–19	20+	
Number of employees							
Over 100	Number	0	0	0	2	1	3.0
	Percentage of group	0.0	0	0	66.7	33.3	100.0
	Percentage of total	0.0	0	0	1.7	0.8	2.5
76–100	Number	0	0	0	4	0	4
	Percentage of group	0.0	0.0	0.0	100.0	0.0	100.0
	Percentage of total	0.0	0.0	0.0	3.3	0.0	3.3
51–75	Number	1	0	0	1	2	4
	Percentage of group	25.0	0.0	0.0	25.0	50.0	100.0
	Percentage of total	0.8	0.0	0.0	0.8	1.7	3.3
26–50	Number	2	1	0	2	7	12
	Percentage of group	16.7	8.3	0.0	16.7	58.3	100.0
	Percentage of total	1.7	0.8	0.0	1.7	5.8	9.9
6–25	Number	7	8	19	19	15	68
	Percentage of group	10.3	11.8	27.9	27.9	22.1	100.0
	Percentage of total	5.8	6.6	15.7	15.7	12.4	56.2
1–5	Number	7	5	8	6	4	30
	Percentage of group	23.3	16.7	26.7	20.0	13.3	100.0
	Percentage of total	5.8	4.1	6.6	5.0	3.3	24.8
Total	Number	17	14	27	34	29	121
	Percentage of group	14.0	11.6	22.3	28.1	24.0	100.0
	Percentage of total	14.0	11.6	22.3	28.1	24.0	100.0

Table A 1.5: Distribution of Businesses (Number of Employees) by Sales Growth in Last Two Years

		Sales growth last year							Total
		No sales	Sales did not grow	Sales grew slowly	Sales grew moderately	Sales grew rapidly	Sales decreased	Not applicable	
Number of employees									
More than 100	Number	0	0	1	1	1	0	0	3
	Percentage of group	0.0	0.0	33.3	33.3	33.3	0.0	0.0	100.0
76–100	Number	0	0	1	3	0	0	0	4
	Percentage of group	0.0	0.0	25.0	75.0	0.0	0.0	0.0	100.0
51–75	Number	0	0	1	3	0	0	0	4
	Percentage of group	0.0	0.0	25.0	75.0	0.0	0.0	0.0	100.0
26–50	Number	0	0	6	3	2	1	0	12
	Percentage of group	0.0	0.0	50.0	25.0	16.7	8.3	0.0	100.0
6–25	Number	0	2	21	34	6	6	0	69
	Percentage of group	0.0	2.9	30.4	49.3	8.7	8.7	0.0	100.0
1–5	Number	1	3	7	13	4	1	2	31
	Percentage of group	3.2	9.7	22.6	41.9	12.9	3.2	6.5	100.0
Total	Number	1	5	37	57	13	8	2	123
	Percentage	0.8	4.1	30.1	46.3	10.6	6.5	1.6	100.0

Table A1.6: Experience in the Management of the Business

		Frequency	Percentage	Valid percentage	Cumulative percentage
	Experience of production				
Valid	Very experienced	42	33.6	36.8	36.8
	Much experience	40	32.0	35.1	71.9
	Reasonable experience	20	16.0	17.5	89.5
	Little or no experience	6	4.8	5.3	94.7
	Some experience	6	4.8	5.3	100.0
	Total	114	91.2	100.0	
Missing	System	11	8.8		
Total		125	100.0		

		Frequency	Percentage	Valid percentage	Cumulative percentage
	Experience of sales and marketing				
Valid	Much experience	59	47.2	48.8	48.8
	Very experienced	27	21.6	22.3	71.1
	Reasonable experience	25	20.0	20.7	91.7
	Some experience	9	7.2	7.4	99.2
	Little or no experience	1	0.8	0.8	100.0
	Total	121	96.8	100.0	
Missing	System	4	3.2		
Total		125	100.0		

		Frequency	Percentage	Valid percentage	Cumulative percentage
	Experience of finance				
Valid	Much experience	49	39.2	39.8	39.8
	Reasonable experience	36	28.8	29.3	69.1
	Very experienced	30	24.0	24.4	93.5
	Some experience	8	6.4	6.5	100.0
	Total	123	98.4	100.0	
Missing	System	2	1.6		
Total		125	100.0		

		Frequency	Percentage	Valid percentage	Cumulative percentage
	Experience of staffing				
Valid	Much experience	54	43.2	45.8	45.8
	Reasonable experience	30	24.0	25.4	71.2
	Very experienced	24	19.2	20.3	91.5
	Some experience	9	7.2	7.6	99.2
	Little or no experience	1	0.8	0.8	100.0
	Total	118	94.4	100.0	
Missing	System	7	5.6		
Total		125	100.0		

Table A1.6: Experience in the Management of the Business (continued)

		Experience of information technology			
		Frequency	Percentage	Valid percentage	Cumulative percentage
Valid	Much experience	39	31.2	32.2	32.2
	Reasonable experience	38	30.4	31.4	63.6
	Very experienced	23	18.4	19.0	82.6
	Some experience	17	13.6	14.0	96.7
	Little or no experience	4	3.2	3.3	100.0
	Total	121	96.8	100.0	
Missing	System	4	3.2		
Total		125	100.0		

		Experience of coping with red tape			
		Frequency	Percentage	Valid percentage	Cumulative percentage
Valid	Much experience	44	35.2	36.7	36.7
	Reasonable experience	35	28.0	29.2	65.8
	Very experienced	26	20.8	21.7	87.5
	Some experience	10	8.0	8.3	95.8
	Little or no experience	5	4.0	4.2	100.0
	Total	120	96.0	100.0	
Missing	System	5	4.0		
Total		125	100.0		

Table A 1.7: Experience of Management by Gender, Start-ups and Rapid Growth Rate

1 = little experience; 5 = very experienced

	Female majority-owned businesses				
Scale	**1**	**2**	**3**	**4**	**5**
Production	11.1%	0.0%	5.6%	22.2%	61.1%
Sales and marketing	0.0%	5.6%	16.7%	33.3%	44.4%
Finance	0.0%	10.5%	26.3%	36.8%	26.3%
Staffing	5.6%	16.7%	16.7%	22.2%	38.9%
Information technology	10.5%	21.1%	31.6%	21.1%	15.8%
Coping with red tape	11.1%	16.7%	22.2%	16.7%	33.3%
	Male majority-owned businesses				
Scale	**1**	**2**	**3**	**4**	**5**
Production	4.9%	6.1%	19.5%	36.6%	32.9%
Sales and marketing	1.2%	8.1%	20.9%	50.0%	19.8%
Finance	0.0%	6.9%	25.3%	40.2%	27.6%
Staffing	0.0%	7.2%	26.5%	49.4%	16.9%
Information technology	2.4%	11.8%	31.8%	31.8%	22.4%
Coping with red tape	3.5%	8.2%	28.2%	38.8%	22.2%
	Start-ups				
Scale	**1**	**2**	**3**	**4**	**5**
Production	0.0%	11.8%	17.6%	35.3%	35.3%
Sales and marketing	5.6%	16.7%	5.6%	38.9%	33.3%
Finance	0.0%	11.1%	27.8%	33.3%	27.8%
Staffing	0.0%	11.1%	22.2%	44.4%	22.2%
Information technology	5.6%	16.7%	27.8%	27.8%	22.2%
Coping with red tape	0.0%	11.8%	52.9%	23.5%	11.8%
	Businesses with rapid growth rate				
Scale	**1**	**2**	**3**	**4**	**5**
Production	0.0%	9.1%	0.0%	54.5%	36.4%
Sales and marketing	7.7%	7.7%	15.4%	61.5%	7.7%
Finance	0.0%	0.0%	23.1%	46.2%	30.8%
Staffing	0.0%	16.7%	16.7%	50.0%	16.7%
Information technology	7.7%	23.1%	15.4%	53.8%	0.0%
Coping with red tape	0.0%	7.7%	30.8%	23.1%	38.5%

Table A2.1: Requests for Finance in Last Three Years by Asset Size of Business

		Assets of business					
		Less than US$100,000	US$100,001–US$200,000	US$200,001–US$500,000	US$500,001–US$1 million	Over US$1 million	Total
Request for finance in last three years							
No	Number	14	11	14	3	3	45
	Percentage of group	41.2	44.0	56.0	20.0	12.5	36.6
	Percentage of total	11.4	8.9	11.4	2.4	2.4	36.6
Yes	Number	20	14	11	12	21	78
	Percentage of group	58.8	56.0	44.0	80.0	87.5	63.4
	Percentage of total	16.3	11.4	8.9	9.8	17.1	63.4
Total	Number	34	25	25	15	24	123
	Percentage of group	100.0	100.0	100.0	100.0	100.0	100.0
	Percentage of total	27.6	20.3	20.3	12.2	19.5	100.0

Table A2.2: Requests for Finance in Last Three Years by Sales Growth Last Year

		Sales growth last year							
		No sales	Sales did not grow	Sales grew slowly	Sales grew moderately	Sales grew rapidly	Sales decreased	Not applicable	Total
Request for finance in last three years									
No	Number	0	3	18	18	4	2	1	46
	Percentage of group	0.0	6.5	39.1	39.1	8.7	4.3	2.2	100.0
Yes	Number	1	2	19	40	9	6	1	78
	Percentage of group	1.3	2.6	24.4	51.3	11.5	7.7	1.3	100.0
Total	Number	1	5	37	58	13	8	2	124
	Percentage of group	8.0	4.0	29.8	46.8	10.5	6.5	1.6	100.0

Table A2.3: Requests for Finance in Last Three Years by Legal Form of Business

		Type of business				
		Private corporation	Public corporation	Sole proprietorship	Partnership	Total
Requests for finance in last three years						
No	Number	26	0	19	1	46
	Percentage of group	56.5	0.0	41.3	2.2	100.0
Yes	Number	50	3	16	9	78
	Percentage of group	64.1	3.8	20.5	11.5	100.0
Total	Number	76	3	35	10	124
	Percentage of group	61.3	2.4	28.2	8.1	100.0

Table A2.4: Types of Finance Requested in Last Three Years

	Demand	Mortgage loan	Long-term loan	New line credit	New credit card	Increase in line of credit limit	Increase in credit card limit
			Number of employees (N = 75)				
1–5	11	3	5	3	1	1	0
6–25	16	10	14	4	2	4	0
26–50	2	1	3	0	1	1	1
51–75	2	0	2	0	0	2	0
76–100	2	2	3	3	3	2	1
Over 100	1	0	0	1	0	2	0
			Turnover (N = 74)				
Under US$100,000	7	2	5	3	1	1	1
US$100,001–US$200,000	9	5	4	1	1	2	0
US$200,001–US$500,000	4	4	4	2	1	3	0
US$500,001–US$1 million	5	1	8	2	2	0	1
Over US$1 million	7	4	6	3	2	6	0
			Sector (N = 76)				
Accounting, computerisation and financial services	3	0	1	1	3	0	0
Agro industry, fisheries and livestock	2	0	3	1	0	1	0
Building material, construction, machinery and manufacturing	0	0	4	1	2	1	0
Distributors	5	3	4	4	2	1	1
Food processing	5	1	2	0	0	3	0

Table A2.4: Types of Finance Requested in Last Three Years (continued)

	Demand	Mortgage loan	Long-term loan	New line credit	New credit card	Increase in line of credit limit	Increase in credit card limit
			Sector (continued)				
Hospitality	1	4	4	0	1	1	0
Pottery, ceramics, glass, jewellery and craft manufacturing	0	1	1	0	0	0	0
Printing publishing, packaging and labelling	3	0	2	0	0	0	0
Services	11	7	6	3	2	3	1
Shipping, storage and warehousing	2	0	0	0	0	0	0
Textiles	0	0	1	0	0	0	0
Wood and metal fabrication	2	0	0	1	0	2	0
			Country (N = 76)				
Antigua	1	0	0	0	0	0	0
Barbados	3	2	4	1	1	0	1
Belize	2	2	8	1	2	2	1
Dominica	0	0	1	1	0	1	0
Grenada	5	3	4	2	1	0	0
Guyana	5	1	1	1	1	4	0
Jamaica	0	0	2	0	0	0	0
St Lucia	3	2	3	2	1	1	0
St Vincent and Tobago	12	4	3	2	1	2	0
			Legal form (N = 76)				
Private Corporation	21	10	20	7	4	7	2
Public Corporation	1	1	0	2	0	1	0
Sole Proprietorship	9	3	6	2	3	1	0
Partnership	3	2	2	0	0	3	0
			Gender (N = 75)				
Male	22	10	20	7	3	11	0
Female	7	2	5	2	2	1	1
Joint	4	4	3	2	2	0	1

Table A2.5: Percentage of Businesses by Number of Employees Requesting Various Types of Financial Products

Employees	1–5	6–25	26–50	51–75	76–100	>100
Demand	64.7	39.0	28.6	50.0	50.0	50.0
Mortgage loan	17.3	24.4	14.3	0.0	50.0	0.0
Long-term loan	29.4	34.1	42.9	50.0	75.0	0.0
New line of credit	17.6	9.8	0.0	0.0	75.0	50.0
New credit card	5.9	4.9	14.35	0.0	75.0	0.0
Increase in line of credit limit	5.9	0.0	14.3	50.0	50.0	100.0
Increase credit card limit	0.0	0.0	14.3	0.0	25.0	0.0

Table A2.6: Percentage of Businesses by Turnover Requesting Various Types of Financial Products

	Over US$1 million	US$500,001– US$1 million	US$200,001– US$500,000	US$100,001– US$200,000	Less than US$100,000
Demand	41.2	41.7	30.8	56.3	43.8
Mortgage loan	23.5	8.3	30.8	31.3	12.5
Long-term loan	35.3	66.7	30.8	25.0	31.3
New line of credit	17.6	16.7	15.4	6.3	18.8
New credit card	11.8	16.7	7.7	6.3	6.3
Increase in line of credit limit	35.3	0.0	23.1	12.5	6.3
Increase credit card limit	0.0	8.3	0.0	0.0	12.5

Table A2.7 New Finance Requested and Authorised in Last Three Years

Finance requested				**Finance authorised**			
	Number in sample	**Number seeking finance**	**Percentage of sample**		**Number in sample**	**Finance authorised**	**Percentage of sample**
Number of Employees (N = 124)				**Number of Employees** (N = 73)			
1–5	32	17	53.1	1–5	14	6	42.9
6–25	69	43	62.3	6–25	40	32	80.0
26–50	12	8	66.7	26–50	9	7	77.8
51–75	4	4	100.0	51–75	4	3	75.0
76–100	4	4	100.0	76–100	4	2	50.0
Over 100	3	2	66.7	Over 100	2	1	50.0
Total	124	78	62.9		73	51	69.8
Turnover (N = 117)				**Turnover** (N = 71)			
Under US$100,000	36	16	44.4	Under US$100,000	14	7	50.0
US$100,001–US$200,000	31	16	51.6	US$100,001–US$200,000	13	10	76.9
US$200,001–US$500,000	15	12	80.0	US$200,001–US$500,000	13	11	84.6
US$500,001–US$1 million	14	12	85.7	US$500,001–US$1 million	12	7	58.3
Over US$1 million	21	19	90.5	Over US$1million	19	13	68.4
Total	117	75	64.15		71	48	67.6
Sector (N = 125)				**Sector** (N = 74)			
Accounting, computerisation and financial services	7	4	57.1	Accounting, computerisation and financial services	4	3	75.0
Agro industry, fisheries and livestock	8	4	50.0	Agro industry, fisheries and livestock	4	2	50.0
Building material, construction, machinery and manufacturing	10	5	50.0	Building material, construction, machinery and manufacturing	5	3	60.0

Table A2.7 New Finance Requested and Authorised in Last Three Years (continued)

Finance requested				**Finance authorised**			
	Number in sample	**Number seeking finance**	**Percentage of sample**		**Number in sample**	**Finance authorised**	**Percentage of sample**
Sector (continued)				**Sector** (continued)			
Distributors	17	11	64.7	Distributors	11	10	90.9
Food processing	16	12	75.0	Food processing	10	7	70.0
Hospitality	14	8	57.1	Hospitality	7	3	42.9
Pottery, ceramics, glass jewellery and craft manufacturing	2	2	100.0	Pottery, ceramics, glass, jewellery and craft manufacturing	2	1	50.0
Printing publishing, packaging and labelling	6	4	66.7	Printing publishing, packaging and labelling	4	4	100.0
Services	37	22	59.5	Services	21	13	61.9
Shipping, storage and warehousing	3	2	66.7	Shipping, storage and warehousing	2	2	100.0
Textiles	1	1	100.0	Textiles	1	0	0.0
Wood and metal fabrication	4	3	75.0	Wood and metal fabrication	3	3	100.0
Total	125	78	62.4	Total	74	51	68.9
Country (N = 125)				**Country** (N = 74)			
Antigua	4	2	50.0	Antigua	3	0	0.0
Barbados	11	7	63.6	Barbados	7	5	71.4
Belize	21	13	61.9	Belize	14	11	78.6
Dominica	9	1	11.1	Dominica	1	0	0.0
Grenada	21	12	57.1	Grenada	10	4	40.0
Guyana	12	8	66.7	Guyana	8	8	100.0
Jamaica	8	3	37.5	Jamaica	3	2	66.7
St Lucia	11	8	72.7	St Lucia	7	4	57.1

Table A2.7 New Finance Requested and Authorised in Last Three Years (continued)

Finance requested				**Finance authorised**			
	Number in sample	**Number seeking finance**	**Percentage of sample**		**Number in sample**	**Finance authorised**	**Percentage of sample**
Country (N = 125)				**Country** (N = 74)			
St Vincent	9	9	100.0	St Vincent	7	4	57.1
Trinidad & Tobago	19	15	78.9	Trinidad and Tobago	14	13	92.9
Total	125	78	62.4		74	51	68.9
Legal form (N =124)				**Legal Form** (N = 74)			
Private corporation	76	50	65.8	Private corporation	47	33	70.2
Public corporation	3	3	100.0	Public corporation	3	3	100.0
Sole proprietorship	35	16	45.7	Sole proprietorship	16	9	56.3
Partnership	10	9	90.0	Partnership	8	6	75.0
Total	124	78	63.7		74	51	68.9
Gender (N = 75)				**Gender** (N = 75)			
Male	89	56	62.9	Male	53	36	67.9
Female	19	11	57.9	Female	11	5	45.5
Joint	15	10	66.7	Joint	9	9	100.0
Total	123	77	62.6	Total	73	50	68.5

Table A2.8: Authorisation of Credit by Asset Size of Business

		Assets of business					
		Less than US$100,000	US$100,001– US$200,000	US$200,001– US$500,000	US$500,001– US$1 million	Over US$1 million	Total
Was credit authorised?							
No	Number	8	3	1	4	7	23
	Percentage of group	47.1	23.1	9.1	33.3	33.3	31.1
	Percentage of total	10.8	4.1	1.4	5.4	9.5	31.1
Yes	Number	9	10	10	8	14	51
	Percentage of group	52.9	76.9	90.9	66.7	66.7	68.9
	Percentage of total	12.2	13.5	13.5	10.8	18.9	68.9
Total	Number	17	13	11	12	21	74
	Percentage of group	100.0	100.0	100.0	100.0	100.0	100.0
	Percentage of total	23.0	17.6	14.9	16.2	28.4	100.0

Table A2.9 Authorisation and Rejection of Finance by Country

		Country of Business										
Was credit authorised?												
		Antigua	Barbados	Belize	Dominica	Grenada	Guyana	Jamaica	St Lucia	St Vincent	Trinidad & Tobago	
No	Number	3	2	3	1	6	0	1	3	3	1	23
	Percentage of group	13.0	8.7	13.0	4.3	26.1	0.0	4.3	13.0	13.0	4.3	100.0
Yes	Number	0	5	11	0	4	8	2	4	4	13	51
	Percentage of group	0.0	9.8	21.6	0.0	7.8	15.7	3.9	7.8	7.8	25.5	100.0
Total	Number	3	7	14	1	10	8	3	7	7	14	74
	Percentage of group	4.1	9.5	18.9	1.4	13.5	10.8	4.1	9.5	9.5	18.9	100.0

Table A2.10: Requests for Finance in Last Three years by Educational Level of Majority Owner

		Educational level of majority owner					
		Primary school	Secondary school	Technical/ vocational	University degree	Post-graduate degree	Total
Requests for finance in last three years							
No	Number	1	5	13	17	9	45
	Percentage of group	2.2	11.1	28.9	37.8	20.0	100.0
Yes	Number	2	18	16	33	9	78
	Percentage of group	2.6	23.1	20.5	42.3	11.5	100.0
Total	Number	3	23	29	50	18	123
	Percentage of group	2.4	18.7	23.6	40.7	14.6	100.0

Table A2.11: Authorisation of Finance by Educational Level of Majority Owner

		Educational level of majority owner					
		Primary school	Secondary school	Technical/ vocational	University degree	Post-graduate degree	Total
Authorisation of credit							
No	Number	1	6	3	10	3	23
	Percentage of group	4.3	26.1	13.0	43.5	13.0	100.0
Yes	Number	1	11	12	23	4	51
	Percentage of group	2.0	21.6	23.5	45.1	7.8	100.0
Total	Number	2	17	15	33	7	74
	Percentage of group	2.7	23.0	20.3	44.6	9.5	100.0

Table A2.12 Authorisation of Finance by Years in Business

		Years in business					
		<3	3–5	6–9	10–19	20+	Total
Authorisation of credit							
No	Number	3	2	7	6	3	21
	Percentage of group	37.5	40.0	41.2	27.3	15.0	29.2
	Percentage of total	4.2	2.8	9.7	8.3	4.2	29.2
Yes	Number	5	3	10	16	17	51
	Percentage of group	62.5	60.0	58.8	72.7	85.0	70.8
	Percentage of total	6.9	4.2	13.9	22.2	23.6	70.8
Total	Number	8	5	17	22	20	72
	Percentage of group	100.0	100.0	100.0	100.0	100.0	100.0
	Percentage of total	11.1	6.9	23.6	30.6	27.8	100.0

Table A2.13: Satisfaction with Service Elements of Financial Institutions

Satisfaction with availability of finance					
		Frequency	Percentage	Valid percentage	Cumulative percentage
Valid	Very satisfied	26	20.8	35.1	35.1
	Somewhat dissatisfied	18	14.4	24.3	59.5
	Satisfied	13	10.4	17.6	77.0
	Very dissatisfied	12	9.6	16.2	93.2
	Dissatisfied	5	4.0	6.8	100.0
	Total	74	59.2	100.0	
Missing	System	51	40.8		
Total		125	100.0		

Satisfaction with range of services					
		Frequency	Percentage	Valid percentage	Cumulative percentage
Valid	Somewhat dissatisfied	24	19.2	32.9	32.9
	Satisfied	20	16.0	27.4	60.3
	Very satisfied	17	13.6	23.3	83.6
	Dissatisfied	8	6.4	11.0	94.5
	Very dissatisfied	4	3.2	5.5	100.0
	Total	73	58.4	100.0	
Missing	System	52	41.6		
Total		125	100.0		

Satisfaction with efficiency of service					
		Frequency	Percentage	Valid percentage	Cumulative percentage
Valid	Somewhat dissatisfied	21	16.8	29.6	29.6
	Satisfied	20	16.0	28.2	57.7
	Very satisfied	17	13.6	23.9	81.7
	Dissatisfied	8	6.4	11.3	93.0
	Very dissatisfied	5	4.0	7.0	100.0
	Total	71	56.8	100.0	
Missing	System	54	43.2		
Total		125	100.0		

Satisfaction with understanding of customers' business needs					
		Frequency	Percentage	Valid percentage	Cumulative percentage
Valid	Somewhat dissatisfied	18	14.4	25.0	25.0
	Satisfied	18	14.4	25.0	50.0
	Very satisfied	18	14.4	25.0	75.0
	Very dissatisfied	10	8.0	13.9	88.9
	Dissatisfied	8	6.4	11.1	100.0
	Total	72	57.6	100.0	
Missing	System	53	42.4		
Total		125	100.0		

Table A2.14: Satisfaction with Service Elements of Financial Institutions by Length of Time Doing Business

		Satisfaction with availability of finance					
		Very dissatisfied	Dissatisfied	Somewhat dissatisfied	Satisfied	Very satisfied	Total
Over 10 years	Number	4	2	8	7	11	32
	Percentage of total	6.7	3.3	13.3	11.7	18.3	53.3
6–10 years	Number	3	1	7	1	4	16
	Percentage of total	5.0	1.7	11.7	1.7	6.7	26.7
0–5 years	Number	2	1	1	1	7	12
	Percentage of total	3.3	1.7	1.7	1.7	11.7	20.0
Total	Number	9	4	16	9	22	60
	Percentage of total	15.0	6.7	26.7	15.0	36.7	100.0
		Satisfaction with range of services					
		Very dissatisfied	**Dissatisfied**	**Somewhat dissatisfied**	**Satisfied**	**Very satisfied**	**Total**
Over 10 years	Number	3	2	10	10	7	32
	Percentage of total	5.0	3.3	16.7	16.7	11.7	53.3
6–10 years	Number	0	2	7	5	2	16
	Percentage of total	0.0	3.3	11.7	8.3	3.3	26.7
0–5 years	Number	0	2	1	4	5	12
	Percentage of total	.0	3.3	1.7	6.7	8.3	20.0
Total	Number	3	6	18	19	14	60
	Percentage of total	5.0	10.0	30.0	31.7	23.3	100.0

Table A2.14: Satisfaction with Service Elements of Financial Institutions by Length of Time doing Business (continued)

		Satisfaction with competence of staff					
		Very dissatisfied	**Dissatisfied**	**Somewhat dissatisfied**	**Satisfied**	**Very satisfied**	**Total**
Over 10 years	Number	2	3	7	10	9	31
	Percentage of total	3.4	5.1	11.9	16.9	15.3	52.5
6–10 years	Number	1	0	8	5	2	16
	Percentage of total	1.7	0.0	13.6	8.5	3.4	27.1
0–5 years	Number	0	2	2	3	5	12
	Percentage of total	0.0	3.4	3.4	5.1	8.5	20.3
Total	Number	3	5	17	18	16	59
	Percentage of total	5.1	8.5	28.8	30.5	27.1	100.0
		Satisfaction with efficiency of service					
		Very dissatisfied	**Dissatisfied**	**Somewhat dissatisfied**	**Satisfied**	**Very satisfied**	**Total**
Over 10 years	Number	2	4	8	8	9	31
	Percentage of total	3.4	6.9	13.8	13.8	15.5	53.4
6 to 10 years	Number	1	0	7	7	1	16
	Percentage of total	1.7	0.0	12.1	12.1	1.7	27.6
0-5 years	Number	0	2	3	2	4	11
	Percentage of total	0.0	3.4	5.2	3.4	6.9	19.0
Total	Number	3	6	18	17	14	58
	Percentage of total	5.2	10.3	31.0	29.3	24.1	100.0

Table A2.14: Satisfaction with Service Elements of Financial Institutions by Length of Time doing Business (continued)

		Satisfaction with understanding of customers' business needs					
		Very dissatisfied	Dissatisfied	Somewhat dissatisfied	Satisfied	Very satisfied	Total
Over 10 years	Number	4	2	8	10	7	31
	Percentage of total	6.8	3.4	13.6	16.9	11.9	52.5
6–10 years	Number	2	4	5	3	2	16
	Percentage of total	3.4	6.8	8.5	5.1	3.4	27.1
0–5 years	Number	1	2	2	2	5	12
	Percentage of total	1.7	3.4	3.4	3.4	8.5	20.3
Total	Number	7	8	15	15	14	59
	Percentage of total	11.9	13.6	25.4	25.4	23.7	100.0

Table A 2.15: Businesses which Did Not Need Finance by Business Characteristics

All businesses	Number	Percentage of sample
Number of employees		
1–5	6	28.6
6–25	12	57.1
26–50	2	9.5
51–75	0	0.0
76–100	0	0.0
Over 100	1	4.8
Total	21	100.0
Turnover		
Under US$100,000	7	35.0
US$100,001–US$200,000	9	45.0
US$200,001–US$500,000	1	5.0
US$500,001–US$1 million	1	5.0
Over US$1 million	2	10.0
Total	20	100.0
Assets		
Under US$100,000	3	14.3
US$100,001–US$200,000	6	28.6
US$200,001–US$500,000	9	42.9
US$500,001–US$1 million	1	4.8
Over US$1 million	2	9.5
Total	21	100.0
Sector		
Accounting, computerisation and financial services	2	9.5
Agro industry, fisheries and livestock	0	0.0
Building material, construction, machinery and manufacturing	2	9.5
Distributors	2	9.5
Food processing	1	4.8
Hospitality	2	9.5
Pottery, ceramics, glass, jewellery and craft manufacturing	0	0.0
Printing, publishing, packaging and labelling	0	0.0
Services	11	52.4
Shipping, storage and warehousing	0	0.0
Textiles	0	0.0
Wood and metal fabrication	1	4.8
Total	21	100.0

Table A 2.15: Businesses which Did Not Need Finance by Business Characteristics
(continued)

All businesses	Number	Percentage of sample
Country		
Antigua	0	0.0
Barbados	1	4.8
Belize	5	23.8
Dominica	8	38.1
Grenada	3	14.3
Guyana	0	0.0
Jamaica	1	4.8
St Lucia	1	4.8
St Vincent	0	0.0
Trinidad & Tobago	2	9.5
Total	21	100.0
Legal form		
Private corporation	15	75.0
Public corporation	0	0.0
Sole proprietorship	5	25.0
Partnership	0	0.0
Total	20	100.0
Gender ownership		
Male	18	90.0
Female	1	5.0
Joint	1	5.0
Total	20	100.0
Origin of business		
Started from scratch	20	95.2
Took over family business	0	0.0
Purchased an existing business	1	4.8
Spin-off from another business	0	0.0
Total	21	100.0
Sales growth last year		
Sales grew moderately	9	42.9
Sales grew slowly	9	42.9
Sales grew rapidly	3	14.3
Sales decreased	0	0.0
Sales did not grow	0	0.0
Total	21	100.0

Table A 2.15: Businesses which Did Not Need Finance by Business Characteristics
(continued)

All businesses	Number	Percentage of sample
Expected future sales growth		
Somewhat stronger	7	33.3
About the same	10	47.6
Much stronger	2	9.5
Somewhat weaker	2	9.5
Much weaker	0	0.0
Total	21	100.0
Original base at home		
Yes	12	60.0
No	6	30.0
N/A	2	10.0
Total	20	100.0
Years in business		
<3 years	4	19.0
3–5 years	2	9.5
6–9 years	5	23.8
10–19 years	6	28.6
Over 20 years	4	19.0
Total	21	100.0

Table A3.1: Sources of Equity Finance

		Frequency	Percentage	Valid percentage	Cumulative percentage
Valid	Friend	9	7.2	52.9	52.9
	Other	4	3.2	23.5	76.5
	Venture capital firm	2	1.6	11.8	88.2
	Private investor	1	0.8	5.9	94.1
	Government agency	1	0.8	5.9	100.0
	Total	17	13.6	100.0	
Missing	System	108	86.4		
Total		125	100.0		

Table A3.2: Equity Finance Declined and Provided by Asset Size of Business

Assets of business		Less than US$100,000	US$100,001– US$200,000	US$200,001– US$500,000	US$500,001– US$1 million	Over US$1 million	Total
Was equity finance provided?							
No	Number	1	0	0	0	2	3
	Percentage of group	33.3	0.0	0.0	0.0	40.0	17.6
	Percentage of total	5.9	0.0	0.0	0.0	11.8	17.6
Yes	Number	2	3	2	4	3	14
	Percentage of group	66.7	100.0	100.0	100.0	60.0	82.4
	Percentage of total	11.8	17.6	11.8	23.5	17.6	82.4
Total	Number	3	3	2	4	5	17
	Percentage of group	100.0	100.0	100.0	100.0	100.0	100.0
	Percentage of total	17.6	17.6	11.8	23.5	29.4	100.0

Table A4.1: Grant or Subsidy Finance Declined and Obtained by Asset Size of Business

Assets of business		Less than US$100,000	US$100,001– US$200,000	US$200,001– US$500,000	US$500,001– US$1 million	Over US$1 million	Total
Was grant or subsidy finance provided?							
No	Number	4	0	1	3	4	12
	Percentage of group	66.7	.0	50.0	100.0	57.1	63.2
	Percentage of total	21.1	.0	5.3	15.8	21.1	63.2
Yes	Number	2	1	1	0	3	7
	Percentage of group	33.3	100.0	50.0	0.0	42.9	36.8
	Percentage of total	10.5	5.3	5.3	0.0	15.8	36.8
Total	Number	6	1	2	3	7	19
	Percentage of group	100.0	100.0	100.0	100.0	100.0	100.0
	Percentage of total	31.6	5.3	10.5	15.8	36.8	100.0

Table A5.1: Organisations Providing the Most Support by Number of Employees

N = 114

Number of employees		1–5	6–25	26–50	51–75	76–100	More than 100	Total
Organisations providing the most support								
Banks	Number	16	37	9	4	1	2	69
	Percentage of group	51.6	59.7	75.0	100.0	33.3	100.0	
Credit unions	Number	17	25	6	2	3	1	54
	Percentage of group	54.8	40.3	50.0	50.0	100.0	50.0	
International donors	Number	12	9	1	1	1	0	24
	Percentage of group	38.7	14.5	8.3	25.0	33.3	0.0	
Local government agencies	Number	4	9	0	1	1	2	17
	Percentage of group	12.9	14.5	0.0	25.0	33.3	100.0	
National government	Number	2	8	1	1	0	1	13
	Percentage of group	6.5	12.9	8.3	25.0	0.0	50.0	
Consulting companies and agencies	Number	3	7	2	0	1	0	13
	Percentage of group	9.7	11.3	16.7	0.0	33.3	0.0	
Large foreign enterprises	Number	1	2	0	0	0	0	3
	Percentage of group	3.2	3.2	0.0	0.0	0.0	0.0	
Service centres	Number	2	0	0	0	0	0	2
	Percentage of group	6.5	0.0	0.0	0.0	0.0	0.0	
Other organisation	Number	2	1	0	1	0	0	4
	Percentage of group	6.5	1.6	0.0	25.0	0.0	0.0	
Total	Number	31	62	12	4	3	2	114
	Percentage of group	27.2	54.4	10.5	3.5	2.6	1.8	100.0

Table A5.2: Organisations Providing the Most Support by Assets

Assets of business		Less than US$100,000	US$100,001–US$200,000	US$200,001–US$500,000	US$500,001–US$1 million	Over US$1 million	Total
Organisations providing the most support							
Banks	Number	19	14	13	4	18	68
	Percentage of group	61.3	58.3	54.2	30.8	85.7	
Credit unions	Number	12	16	9	6	12	55
	Percentage of group	38.7	66.7	37.5	46.2	57.1	
International donors	Number	11	4	8	0	2	25
	Percentage of group	35.5	16.7	33.3	0.0	9.5	
Local government agencies	Number	6	1	2	4	4	17
	Percentage of group	19.4	4.2	8.3	30.8	19.0	
National government	Number	2	1	7	1	2	13
	Percentage of group	6.5	4.2	29.2	7.7	9.5	
Consulting companies and agencies	Number	2	2	6	2	1	13
	Percentage of group	6.5	8.3	25.0	15.4	4.8	
Large foreign enterprises	Number	1	2	0	0	0	3
	Percentage of group	3.2	8.3	0.0	0.0	0.0	
Service centres	Number	0	2	0	0	0	2
	Percentage of group	0.0	8.3	0.0	0.0	0.0	
Other organisations	Number	0	1	1	1	1	4
	Percentage of group	0.0	4.2	4.2	7.7	4.8	
Total	Number	31	24	24	13	21	113
	Percentage of group	27.4	21.2	21.2	11.5	18.6	100.0

Table A5.3: Areas of Assistance Required by Assets

Assets of business		Less than US$100,000	US$100,001– US$200,000	US$200,001– US$500,000	US$500,001– US$1 million	Over US$1 million	Total
Areas in which assistance was needed in making an application							
Preparation of a feasibility study on the business project	Number	19	10	14	5	14	62
Information on markets and marketing requirements	Number	15	10	8	8	9	50
Preparation of a business plan	Number	14	10	7	3	8	42
Preparation and maintenance of financial records	Number	10	11	11	5	4	41
Information on what is required to fulfil the conditions for the loan	Number	10	12	7	5	7	41
Preparation of the application for finance	Number	10	9	9	5	6	39
Other	Number	1	0	0	0	1	2
Total	Number	28	22	22	12	21	105

Table A5.4: Areas of Assistance Required by Educational Level of Owner

		Educational level of majority owner					
		Primary school	Secondary school	Technical/ vocational	University degree	Post-graduate degree	Total
Area in which assistance required							
Preparation of the application for finance	Number	2	10	9	14	3	38
	Percentage of group	66.7	52.6	34.6	33.3	20.0	
Preparation and maintenance of financial records	Number	1	8	11	18	2	40
	Percentage of group	33.3	42.1	42.3	42.9	13.3	
Information on markets and marketing requirements	Number	1	10	10	21	7	49
	Percentage of group	33.3	52.6	38.5	50.0	46.7	
Information on what is required to fulfil the conditions for the loan	Number	1	4	13	17	5	40
	Percentage of group	33.3	21.1	50.0	40.5	33.3	
Preparation of a business plan	Number	1	10	12	14	5	42
	Percentage of group	33.3	52.6	46.2	33.3	33.3	
Preparation of a feasibility study on the business project	Number	1	13	14	26	8	62
	Percentage of group	33.3	68.4	53.8	61.9	53.3	
Other	Number	0	0	1	0	1	2
	Percentage of group	0.0	0.0	3.8	0.0	6.7	
Total	Number	3	19	26	42	15	105

Table A5.5: Knowledge of Loan Evaluation Criteria

		Frequency	Percentage
Valid	No	67	53.6
	Yes	46	36.8
	Total	113	90.4
Missing	System	11	8.8
	No response	1	0.8
	Total	12	9.6
Total		125	100.0

Table A5.6: Most Appropriate Form of Finance by Number of Employees

		Most appropriate finance for business								
		Demand or short-term loan	Overdraft facilities	Long-term loan	Lease of equipment or machinery	Line of credit	Credit card limit	Equity finance	Other	Total
Number of employees										
1–5	Number	10	12	20	5	12	4	5	0	31
	Percentage of group	32.3	38.7	64.5	16.1	38.7	12.9	16.1	0.0	
6–25	Number	20	40	42	6	21	15	8	2	67
	Percentage of group	29.9	59.7	62.7	9.0	31.3	22.4	11.9	3.0	
26–50	Number	4	7	6	1	5	2	1	0	12
	Percentage of group	33.3	58.3	50.0	8.3	41.7	16.7	8.3	0.0	
51–75	Number	2	3	3	0	2	1	0	0	4
	Percentage of group	50.0	75.0	75.0	0.0	50.0	25.0	0.0	0.0	
76–100	Number	0	3	4	2	4	1	1	0	4
	Percentage of group	0.0	75.0	100.0	50.0	100.0	25.0	25.0	0.0	
Over 100	Number	2	1	1	0	2	0	0	0	3
	Percentage of group	66.7	33.3	33.3	0.0	66.7	0.0	0.0	0.0	
Total	Number	38	66	76	14	46	23	15	2	121

Appendix 3

Financial Institutions

Table A1.1: Types of Finance Provided to SMEs

	Responses		Percentage of cases
	N	Percentage	
Types of finance provided to SMEs			
Demand or short-term loan	28	22.8	96.6
Mortgage loan	21	17.1	72.4
New line of credit (also called operating loan)	18	14.6	62.1
Increase in the credit limit of current lines of credit	18	14.6	62.1
Long-term loan (loan for a term of ten years or more)	14	11.4	48.3
New credit card	11	8.9	37.9
Increase in the credit limit of current credit cards	10	8.1	34.5
Royalty-based loan	3	2.4	10.3
Total	123	100.0	

Table A1.2: Proportion of Loans Requested by SMEs.

	N	Minimum	Maximum	Sum	Mean
Demand or short-term loan	23	10	100	1336	58.09
Long-term loan	15	1	80	433	28.87
Mortgage loan	14	1	45	219	15.64
New line of credit	11	1	30	157	14.27
Increase in the credit limit	10	1	20	97	9.70
New credit card	8	1	10	40	5.00
Increase in the credit limit	7	1	10	27	3.86
Other type of debt finance	5	3	100	146	29.20
Royalty-based loan	1	20	20	20	20.00

Table A1.3: Long-term Finance Provided to SMEs in Local Currency by Type of Financial Institution

		Does company provide long-term finance to SMEs in local currency		
		No	**Yes**	**Total**
Type of financial institution				
Commercial bank	Number	5	10	15
	Percentage of group	33.3	66.7	100.0
Other financial institution	Number	4	3	7
	Percentage of group	57.1	42.9	100.0
International or regional financial institution	Number	0	1	1
	Percentage of group	0.0	100.0	100.0
Government agency	Number	1	1	2
	Percentage of group	50.0	50.0	100.0
Credit union	Number	3	1	4
	Percentage of group	75.0	25.0	100.0
Total	Number	13	16	29
	Percentage of group	44.8	55.2	100.0

Table A1.4: Type of Businesses Requesting Finance

	Responses		Percentage of cases
	N	Percentage	
Types of businesses requesting finance			
Agriculture (sugar, market vegetables, flowers)	28	14.5	87.5
Fisheries (including live fish for aquariums)	22	11.4	68.8
Tourism (hotels, resorts, and supporting activities)	26	13.5	81.3
Food processing/food franchises	26	13.5	81.3
Clothing and footwear manufacture	14	7.3	43.8
Aquaculture (farming of fish, prawns, etc.)	9	4.7	28.1
Forestry (logs, sawn timber and wood products)	10	5.2	31.3
Financial, marketing, scientific, packaging services to exporters	8	4.1	25.0
Data-processing centres	8	4.1	25.0
Call Centres for customer-response services	8	4.1	25.0
Residential tertiary education aimed at third country nationals	8	4.1	25.0
Medical treatment or recuperation facilities for overseas patients	6	3.1	18.8
Mineral extraction (gold, diamonds, sea salt, etc.)	5	2.6	15.6
Assembly of electrical and electronic equipment	2	1.0	6.3
Assembly of vehicles	2	1.0	6.3
Other business	11	5.7	34.4
Total	193	100.0	

Table A1.5: Mean and Modal Minimum Requests for Finance by SMEs

Sector	Mean	Mode	Sum
Tourism (hotels, resorts and supporting activities)	$43,592.19	$7,200	$697,475
Fisheries (including live fish for aquariums)	$42,896.00	$1,800	$643,440
Financial, marketing, scientific, packaging services to exporters	$23,240.00	$3,600	$116,200
Forestry (logs, sawn timber and wood products)	$18,220.00	$2,500	$163,980
Call Centres for customer-response services	$17,000.00	$8,000[a]	$51,000
Food processing/food franchise	$11,877.86	$3,600	$166,290
Clothing and footwear manufacture	$11,554.44	$3,600	$103,990
Data-processing centres	$10,733.33	$3,600	$32,200
Agriculture (sugar, market vegetables, flowers)	$6,849.75	$1,000	$136,995
Assembly of electrical and electronic equipment	$5,250.00	$500[a]	$10,500
Mineral extraction (gold, diamonds, sea-salt, etc.)	$4,725.00	$400[a]	$18,900
Aquaculture (farming of fish, prawns, etc.)	$2,928.57	$2,500	$20,500
Medical treatment or recuperation facilities for overseas patients	$2,790.00	$3,600	$11,160
Residential tertiary education aimed at third country nationals	$2,100.00	$1,800[a]	$4,200
Other business	$9,471.88	$75[a]	$75,775

[a]Multiple modes exist. The smallest value is shown.

Table A1.6: Mean and Modal Maximum Requests for Finance by SMEs

Sector	Mean	Mode	Sum
Financial, marketing, scientific, packaging services to exporters	$692,000.00	$18,000[a]	$3,460,000
Forestry (logs, sawn timber and wood products)	$571,125.00	$25,000	$4,569,000
Clothing and footwear manufacture	$392,688.89	$36,000	$3,534,200
Tourism (hotels, resorts and supporting activities)	$332,288.24	$288,000	$5,648,900
Food processing/food franchise	$312,233.33	$20,000	$5,620,200
Call Centres for customer-response services	$222,400.00	$17,000[a]	$1,112,000
Aquaculture (farming of fish, prawns, etc.)	$190,644.44	$50,000	$1,715,800
Agriculture (sugar, market vegetables, flowers)	$149,913.64	$8,000	$3,298,100
Fisheries (including live fish for aquariums)	$83,913.33	$10,000[a]	$1,258,700
Assembly of electrical and electronic equipment	$33,000.00	$3,500[a]	$66,000
Data-processing centres	$29,750.00	$18,000	$119,000
Mineral extraction (gold, diamonds, sea-salt, etc.)	$26,480.00	$25,000	$132,400
Residential tertiary education aimed at third country nationals	$21,133.33	$9,000[a]	$63,400
Medical treatment or recuperation facilities for overseas patients	$12,600.00	$18,000	$37,800

[a]Multiple modes exist. The smallest value is shown.

Table A1.7: Tenors of Loans Typically Requested by SMEs

Sector	Mean	Median	Mode	Minimum	Maximum	Sum
Assembly of vehicles	10.00	10.00	10	10	10	10
Tourism (hotels, resorts and supporting activities)	8.39	7.50	10	3	20	151
Financial, marketing, scientific, packaging services to exporters	8.00	10.00	10	5	10	40
Food processing/food franchise	7.59	5.00	5[a]	1	30	129
Residential tertiary education aimed at third country nationals	7.00	8.00	10[a]	3	10	21
Forestry (logs, sawn timber and wood products)	6.67	7.50	10	2	10	40
Call Centres for customer-response services	6.00	5.00	5	4	10	24
Agriculture (sugar, market vegetables, flowers)	5.29	5.00	5	1	10	111
Clothing and footwear manufacture	5.00	5.00	5	1	10	45
Medical treatment or recuperation facilities for overseas patients	5.00	5.00	7[a]	3	7	15
Fisheries (including live fish for aquariums)	4.14	4.50	5	2	6	58
Assembly of electrical and electronic equipment	4.00	4.00	4	4	4	4
Data-processing centres	4.00	3.00	3	3	6	12
Mineral extraction (gold, diamonds, sea-salt, etc.)	3.50	4.00	5	1	5	14
Aquaculture (farming of fish, prawns, etc.)	3.38	3.00	3	1	5	27

[a]Multiple modes exist. The smallest value is shown.

Table A2.1: Percentage of Applications for Long-term Finance Declined by Sector

Sector	Mean	Mode	Sum
Agriculture (sugar, market vegetables, flowers)	34.29	20	240
Fisheries (including live fish for aquariums)	55.00	20[a]	220
Aquaculture (farming of fish, prawns, etc.)	20.00	20	20
Forestry (logs, sawn timber and wood products)	20.00	20	20
Tourism (hotels, resorts and supporting activities)	35.00	40	245
Mineral extraction (gold, diamonds, sea-salt, etc.)	10.00	10	10
Residential tertiary education aimed at third country nationals	6.67	5	20
Medical treatment or recuperation facilities for overseas patients	5.00	0[a]	10
Data-processing centres	25.00	20[a]	50
Call Centres for customer-response services	40.00	0[a]	120
Financial, marketing, scientific, packaging services to exporters	46.67	20[a]	140
Clothing and footwear manufacture	25.00	20[a]	100
Food processing/food franchise	31.88	20	255

[a]Multiple modes exist. The smallest value is shown.

Table A2.2: Best Estimate of the Rate of Failure of Business Loans

		Frequency	Percentage	Valid percentage	Cumulative percentage
Valid	5–9%	12	37.5	42.9	42.9
	Under 5%	7	21.9	25.0	67.9
	15–20%	4	12.5	14.3	82.1
	10–14%	3	9.4	10.7	92.9
	Actual %	2	6.3	7.1	100.0
	Total	28	87.5	100.0	
Missing	System	4	12.5		
Total		32	100.0		

References

Fraser, Stuart (2004). *Finance for Small and Medium Sized Enterprises – A Report on the 2004 UK Study of SME Finances*. Centre for Small and Medium-Sized Enterprises, Warwick Business School, University of Warwick.

Harvie, C. and Lee, B.C (2002). 'The Role of SMEs in National Economics in East Asia', in *East Asian SMEs: Contemporary Issues and Developments – An Overview*. Edward Elgar Publishing Ltd.

Heidrick, Ted R. and Keddie, Russell R. (2002). *Equity Financing Alternatives for Small Businesses: A Review of Best Practices in the United States*. Report prepared for Industry Canada.

Hughes, Anthony and Brewster, Havelock (2002). *Lowering the Threshold – Reducing the Cost and Risk of Private Direct investment in Least Developed, Small and Vulnerable Economies*. Commonwealth Secretariat.

Industry Canada (2002, 2003). *Small and Medium-sized Enterprise Financing in Canada.*

Japanese Small and Medium Enterprise Agency. *Best Practices for Small and Medium-size Enterprises. http://www.chusho.meti.go.jp/sme_english/index.html*

Statistics Canada (2003). *Survey on Financing of Small and Medium Enterprises*. Small Business and Special Survey Division, 2001.

Statistics Canada in partnership with Industry Canada and the Department of Finance (2004). *Survey of Suppliers of Business Financing.*

Wesley, Glenn D. (2005). *Microfinance in the Caribbean: How to go Further*. Inter-American Development Bank.

World Bank. *Enterprise Development Strategy – Small and Medium-sized Enterprises.*